What's in a Name? Assessing Mission Studies Program Titles

What's In A Name? Assessing Mission Studies Program Titles
The 2015 Proceedings of the Association of Professors of Missions.

Published by First Fruits Press, © 2015
Digital version at http://place.asburyseminary.edu/academicbooks/12/

ISBN: 9781621714705 (print),
9781621714422 (digital), 9781621715641 (kindle)

For all other uses, contact
Association of Professors of Missions
108 W. High St.
Lexington, KY 40507
http://www.asmweb.org/content/apm

What's In A Name? Assessing Mission Studies Program Titles
The 2015 Proceedings of the Association of Professors of Missions.
(vi, 221 pages : illustrations ; 21 cm.)
Wilmore, Ky. : First Fruits Press, ©2014.
ISBN-13: 9781621714705 (pbk.)
1. Missions – Study and teaching – Congresses. 2. Missions – Theory – Congresses. 3. Education – Philosophy – Congresses. 4. Teaching – Methodology – Congresses. I. Title. II. Danielson, Robert A. (Robert Alden), 1969- III. Hartley, Benjamin L. (Benjamin Loren) IV. Association of Professors of Mission annual meeting (2014 : St. Paul, Minn.) V. Association of Professors of Mission. VI. The 2014 proceedings of the Association of Professors of Missions.
BV2020 .A876 2014

Cover design by Jon Ramsey

APM

What's in a Name?

Assessing Mission Studies Program Titles

The 2015 proceedings of
The Association of Professors of Missions

Edited by
Robert A. Danielson
Larry W. Caldwell

2015 APM Annual Meeting
Weaton, Illinois
June 18 - 19, 2015

First Fruits Press
The Academic Open Press of Asbury Theological Seminary
204 N. Lexington Ave., Wilmore, KY 40390
859-858-2236
first.fruits@asburyseminary.edu
asbury.to/firstfruits

About the Association of Professors of Mission

ROBERT DANIELSON, ADVISORY COMMITTEE MEMBER

The Association of Professors of Mission (APM) was formed in 1952 at Louisville, Kentucky and was developed as an organization to focus on the needs of people involved in the classroom teaching of mission studies. However, the organization also challenged members to be professionally involved in scholarly research and share this research through regular meetings. In the 1960's Roman Catholic scholars and scholars from conservative Evangelical schools joined the conciliar Protestants who initially founded the organization.

With the discussion to broaden membership to include other scholars from areas like anthropology, sociology, and linguistics who were actively engaged in mission beyond the teaching profession, the decision was made to found the American Society of Missiology (ASM) in 1972. Since the importance of working with mission educators was still vital, the APM continued as a separate organization, but always met in conjunction with the ASM at their annual meetings.

The APM continues as a professional society of those interested in the teaching of mission from as wide an ecumenical spectrum as possible. As an organization it works to help and support those who teach mission, especially those who often lack a professional network to help mentor and guide them in this task. Through its influence, the APM has also helped establish the prominence and scholarly importance of the academic discipline of missiology throughout theological education.

Table of Contents

Conference Proceedings

Foreword

J. NELSON JENNINGS

What's in a Name?

Assessing Mission Studies Program Titles

The June 2015 Annual Meeting of the Association of Professors of Mission examined the titles that educational institutions, North American and otherwise, use for their mission studies programs. Over recent decades many seminaries and colleges, perhaps most notably Fuller Theological Seminary, have switched from using program titles that contain the term mission(s) to social science labels, e.g., intercultural studies. Various religious labels have also been used, e.g., the more recently developing discipline of world Christianity.

These nomenclature shifts have affected students and graduates in such important ways as personal security. That particular factor catalyzed Fuller, especially in the wake of the September 11, 2001 attacks, to move forward in changing its School of World Mission to the School of Intercultural Studies. As Betsy Glanville's fascinating paper points out, however, that change was neither simple nor easy. Delicate institutional, historical, personal, and other concerns entered into the picture. As the presence of a sizeable number of Fuller-related participants at the APM meeting indicated, the change at Fuller was widely felt and pacesetting.

In addition to security concerns, how the titles of mission studies programs have affected institutions' recruitment of students and new faculty has also been an important area of consideration. Implications for a program's curriculum – whether undergraduate, graduate, or postgraduate – as well as possibly for an institution's other programs is yet another major factor. An institution's desired outcomes for its mission studies program relate to the title employed. The related type of degree that is earned, e.g., DMiss, DMin, PhD, ThD, MTh/ThM, enters the picture as well.

The theme proved stimulating and constructive for conference participants, and the papers presented here should do the same for readers. The net effect is that the studies here cast fresh light on how educators understand their various relationships to the *missio Dei* in today's ever-transitioning Christian world mission movement.

J. Nelson Jennings

2015 APM President

Conference Theme

Association of Professors of Mission

Annual Meeting

18-19 June 2015

Wheaton College, Wheaton, IL

What's in a Name?

Assessing Mission Studies Program Titles

For full details please visit the APM web page at

www.asmweb.org/content/apm

The 2015 Annual Meeting of the APM will examine the titles that educational institutions, North American and otherwise, use for their mission studies programs. Many seminaries and colleges have switched from using program titles that contain the term mission(s) to social science labels, e.g., intercultural studies, or to different religious labels, e.g., the more recently developing discipline of world Christianity. These nomenclature shifts affect students and graduates in such important ways as personal security or employability. What the titles mean for how institutions recruit students and new faculty is also an important area of consideration. Implications for a program's curriculum – whether undergraduate, graduate, or postgraduate – as well as possibly for an institution's other programs also merit assessment. An institution's desired outcomes for its mission studies program relate to the title employed. The related type of degree that is earned, e.g., DMiss, DMin, PhD, ThD, MTh/ThM, enters the picture as well. The examination of these and other related areas should cast fresh light on how educators understand their various relationships to the *missio Dei* in today's ever-transitioning Christian world mission movement.

Persons interested in presenting papers may submit a proposed title with a 150-200 word abstract and a 30 word bio to APM president Nelson Jennings at *jennings@omsc.org* by February 13, 2015.

APM

Plenary Papers

Name Change at Fuller's School of World Mission to School of Intercultural Studies

ELIZABETH "BETSY" GLAINVILLE, PHD

DOI: 10.7252/Paper. 000048

About the Author

Elizabeth "Betsy" Glanville (PhD Fuller Theological Seminary) is Senior Faculty of Leadership in the School of Intercultural Studies, Fuller Theological Seminary. She has recently retired after fifteen years as Director of the Doctoral Programs and Admin-Faculty. She continues to teach in the Doctor of Missiology (Doctor of Intercultural Studies) program. Her studies include women in leadership, leadership development, research design and methods. She was part of the faculty and administration as they worked through the name change from School of World Mission to School of Intercultural Studies. She is currently on the Advisory Council for APM.

Introduction

What's in a name? Can it be the power of life or death? Opportunity or closed doors or imprisonment? Hope or disillusionment? As Fuller's School of World Mission changed its name to School of Intercultural Studies, we encountered all of the above to some degree or another. This paper follows the journey of the name change process, looking at various factors that drove the process as well as the hurdles that had to be overcome. I will use two leadership theories that will help frame the process and give understanding to the significance of certain steps and decisions along the way.

Theoretical Frames

Ronald A. Heifetz and Marty Linsky introduced the concepts of technical change in contrast to adaptive change.[1] Technical change is applying current knowledge and know-how to solve a problem and can usually be easily done. Adaptive change requires new learning, culture change, and new ways of working. Change might require new habits, new beliefs, new priorities, or new loyalties. Because this kind of change requires people at all levels of an organization to think and act differently about a situation or a problem to be solved, the opportunity for leadership failure is greater, and the challenges are compounded.[2]

---

1   Heifetz, Ronald A. and Marty Linsky. 2002. *Leadership on the Line: Staying Alive through the Dangers of Leading*. Boston, MA: Harvard Business School. See also Heifetz, Ronald A, Alexander Grashow, and Marty Linsky. 2009. *The Practice of Adaptive Leadership: Tools and Tactics for Changing Your Organization and the World. Boston*, MA: Harvard Business School.

2   Heifetz and Linsky, p. 1.

School of World Mission and Institute of Church Growth became SWM (pronounced "swim"), gradually, over the years, dropping Institute of Church Growth in the everyday use of our name (though it was still officially part of our name as some senior faculty would periodically remind us). This had been a gradual technical change. However, changing both School of World Mission and Institute of Church Growth to something else proved to be an adaptive challenge that meant a complete paradigm shift for many navigating complex adaptive changes. This concept of an adaptive *challenge* or adaptive *change* is one frame for understanding the name change process at Fuller.

The second theoretical frame comes from Lee G. Bolman and Terrance E. Deal who introduce the concept of four frames that help a leader analyze and view an organizational structure from different perspectives.[3] The four frames are Structural, Human Resource, Political, and Symbolic.

These frames will help us see the hurdles and why they were so important to address along the way. For lasting change to happen, the political and symbolic frames are the most likely to become critical hurdles and are the ones that are in focus for this paper.

A leader ignores the political frame at their own risk. The informal power coalitions have the potential to undermine or derail any change process and blindside a leader who is unaware of their power and/or has not built allies in the change process. The political powers are not necessarily negative forces, but their presence must be recognized and can be used for positive results, or, if ignored, can totally derail a change effort.[4]

The symbolic frame describes the anchors that hold an institution or group on track. These include things like vision, rituals, symbols, history, and stories that define the institution.[5] For SWM these included things like the commitment to missions, to training those who would be working with unreached peoples around the world, and McGavran's missiology and church growth. We have a history of scholar-practitioners—faculty who have been on the mission field, bringing significant first-hand experience

---

3   Bolman, Lee G. and Terrence E. Deal. 2008. *Reframing Organizations: Artistry, Choice, and Leadership.* 4th edition. San Francisco, CA: Jossey-Bass.

4   Bolman and Deal, pp. 194-195.

5   Bolman and Deal, pp. 253-254.

along with their scholarly studies and on-going research to the academic context. We needed to be sure that any change did not lose these historical anchors and clearly provided continuity with our original vision.

The Initial Pressures for Change

The initial impetus for change came from our alums who were serving in closed countries (most frequently Muslim contexts) including the Arab world, communist countries, China, and Indonesia. Dudley Woodberry, our Professor of Islamic Studies and Dean from 1993-1999, was receiving regular reports of visas being denied, revoked, or not renewed if they referenced their SWM degrees because of the word "mission" in their school names and /or degrees. Their other option was to not mention the school and degree at all, which then lessened their credentials in a visa application process.

During the 1990s and early 2000s, we received a steady stream and an increasing number of such reports. The ultimate example was an alum who had been given permission to start a training institute in an Arab country, only to have it revoked and then given 24 hours to leave the country when his credentials were reviewed and his SWM degree was discovered with the word "mission" in it. At that point, for Woodberry, the need for the name change was absolutely imperative and the sooner the better.[6]

When Sherwood Lingenfelter became Dean of SWM in 1999, he got permission to use a DBA of School of Intercultural Studies as an alternate diploma. This worked as long as the visa-issuing embassies only looked at the paper diploma and did not investigate the Fuller web site which clearly named the school as School of World Mission. Thus it quickly became clear that the simple structural change was not the permanent solution, and, at best, only a temporary band aid.[7]

---

6   Email from Lingenfelter to SWM faculty, October 2, 2002

7   Interview with Sherwood Lingenfelter, June 1, 2015.

Then the attacks of 9/11 became the ultimate tipping point and created both a new interest in Islamic studies, mission to the Muslims, as well as the critical awareness of the word "mission" in our name creating a barrier to even being able to access Muslim contexts.

Step One: Agreement among the SWM Faculty

In the fall of 2001, the faculty, began discussions under Lingenfelter's direction. Though conversations were on-going from the previous years, they took on a new urgency after 9/11. As part of gathering both information and support for the name change process, Lingenfelter authorized a survey sent to all SWM graduates. The response was generally in favor of the name change: 151 of 204 responses said "yes" to the name change, with a wide variety of suggestions for a new name.[8]

By the winter of 2002, most agreed that the name should be changed, but we could not agree on changed to what?? A committee was established to create some guidelines for the name change, including tenured faculty: Charles Van Engen, Dudley Woodberry, Wilbert Shenk, and Eddie Gibbs.[9] Initially, as we looked at possible names, we were looking at names that seemed to be unique, that would enable us to continue to stand out as a flagship school training those who were seeking a career in missions. We looked at names, but we had no agreement as most of them seemed too narrow and thus did not really describe the totality of who we were, or were too similar to secular business or international programs.

In May, Lingenfelter told us that the window of opportunity was probably closing—we needed to make a decision and move the process forward to the Faculty Senate, Joint Faculty, and the Board of Trustees.

---

8   Six Hundred graduates were contacted, with 204 responses. Some of the suggested names included: School of Intercultural Communications, School of Global Studies (or Service), School of Intercultural Studies, School of World Religions, McGavran School of Intercultural Studies, School of Intercultural Theological Studies, School of Non-Western Religions and Cultures, and more.

9   The guidelines included: 1. Not too missional so graduates can work in creative access contexts. 2. An honest description of something(s) we do. 3. As inclusive of all we do as expedient. 4. Academically appropriate. 5. (Of lesser importance but a plus, if it could have a hint of mission, incarnation, or crossing barriers).

Otherwise we would have to wait another five years or more. At that meeting, Chuck Kraft suggested that what we really needed was a name that would allow us to go "under the radar" and not stand out. It was one of those "Aha" moments that caught everyone's attention. Before we were through we were in agreement to put forth the name School of Intercultural Studies, the same name being used by Biola and other schools.

At our October, 2002, Faculty Meeting, the motion was passed to put forward the name of School of Intercultural Studies which was already reflected in the name of various degrees, e.g. Masters of Intercultural Studies, and PhD in Intercultural Studies.[10]

At this point the "push" factors were the challenges that our alums were facing that were hindering their ability to do the work of mission in the creative access countries and Muslim contexts. The initial resistance came from older faculty who had been at the school for 15-25 years, and were not particularly impacted in their mission contexts by these kinds of visa restrictions and denials. A number could be described as "neutral" and so were open to considering the possibility of a name change, and were eventually persuaded. But this process took a good six months of ongoing discussions both in and outside of faculty gatherings.

The next hurdle was the rest of the Seminary and the Board of Trustees. The requested name change went through the Seminary channels pretty quickly, but the Board of Trustees proved challenging.[11]

Step Two: Approval from the Board of Trustees

In November, 2002, the request was presented to the Academic Affairs Committee of the Board of Trustees, and approved to be presented to the entire Board.[12] However at the Board meeting, the vote, while it passed, was so close that the Chair of the Board made the decision to table the final vote until further background research could be presented.[13] This was

10   SWM Faculty Minutes, October 8, 2002.

11   Approved by Faculty Senate on October 15, 2002, and Joint Faculty on October 22, 2002.

12   Minutes from the Board of Trustees, Academic Committee-School of World Missions, November 11, 2002.

13   Interview with Lingenfelter, June 1, 2015.

a major, unexpected hurdle. Suddenly it was clear that this was not going to be as easy a decision process as everyone had hoped for and had anticipated. There were some very strong voices on the Board against the name change. This was clearly now an adaptive challenge that needed careful guidance to proceed. From the perspective of the Political Frame, this decision proved to be well-grounded. Time allowed for greater unity to be built and bring the Board together in support of the decision, keeping unity in the Board.[14]

Thus in January 2003, C. Douglas McConnell, as the Dean-elect, to take office in March 2003, was given the mandate to shepherd the name change process through the Board of Trustees. As Lingenfelter noted, McConnell could speak from the perspective of the mission world, because he came from the position of International Director of Pioneers. McConnell also brought significant experience in leadership and leadership change. Furthermore, because Lingenfelter was both Provost and Acting Dean, he did not have the time and flexibility in his schedule to do the necessary work to gather the needed votes among the trustees.[15]

Figure 1: January 2003 Progress Analysis

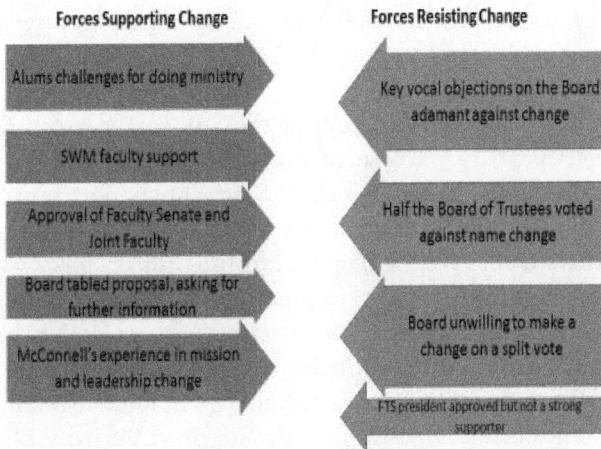

Forces Supporting Change

- Alums challenges for doing ministry
- SWM faculty support
- Approval of Faculty Senate and Joint Faculty
- Board tabled proposal, asking for further information
- McConnell's experience in mission and leadership change

Forces Resisting Change

- Key vocal objections on the Board adamant against change
- Half the Board of Trustees voted against name change
- Board unwilling to make a change on a split vote
- FTS president approved but not a strong supporter

---

14   Ibid.

15   Ibid.

Figure 1 provides a visual picture of the forces for and against change as of January 2003. The biggest factors to deal with were the Board's unwillingness to act on a split decision and the vocal, adamant opposition to the name change on the Board. The continued open door for change was in the willingness of the Board to table the proposal, rather than reject it, and to hear further support for the name change. The background and role of McConnell became critical to the next steps.

McConnell's background included leadership and change dynamics. So, working with the Chair of the Board of Trustees, he began to contact a group of key trustees to both understand their issues and to work towards building a coalition for change. McConnell describes several key people he worked with: one was very supportive and became a key mentor in understanding the Board and the Board processes, but another was a key opponent of the name change who was a strong, vocal, and persuasive voice on the Board. McConnell's goal was to build enough of a supportive coalition from Board members so that those who were neutral could be persuaded, and that even if strong adamant voices could not be persuaded, their ability to control the vote could be minimized.

At the March 2003 Board meeting, an Ad Hoc SWM Name Change Committee had been formed, and worked to identify the primary constituencies (SWM faculty; students, graduates, and supporters; mission organizations and movements, and the larger world), and their concerns. McConnell was able to frame the name change in terms of entrance and access to contexts for mission, countering the concern that we were moving away from our primary purpose of mission. Using a well-documented presentation, McConnell was also able to present support from previous Deans, particularly Paul Pierson and Woodberry, key faculty, and graduates. Several alternate names were discussed, but the primary focus was on the School of Intercultural Studies. He reported that the committee would bring a proposal for a vote at the June meeting, with a plan for the roll out of the new name connected with the installation of McConnell as the new Dean in Fall 2003.[16] Figure 2 shows the change in forces working for and against the name change. The strongest force against the name change was

---

16   Board of Trustee Minutes, March 10-11, 2003. The final approval was passed. Minutes, June 12-13, 2003.

some continued, but limited, vocal objections from those who still thought this name change was moving away from the initial and primary purpose of the school related to mission.

Step Three: Roll Out of the New Name

With approval of the name change to School of Intercultural Studies (SIS), the next challenge was how to communicate this to all the constituents. Fuller did not have a Marketing Department then as we do now, so the responsibility for spreading the news was in the hands of McConnell and the SIS Dean's office.[17] McConnell and the faculty developed a list of "Talking Points" to help communicate the reasons behind the name change.[18] The central theme was to stress that the new name would enable us to do the same purpose and goals we have always done, but to be able to do it in a way that allows people to have access to otherwise closed or limited access contexts in order to share the Gospel

Figure 2: June 2003 Final Vote

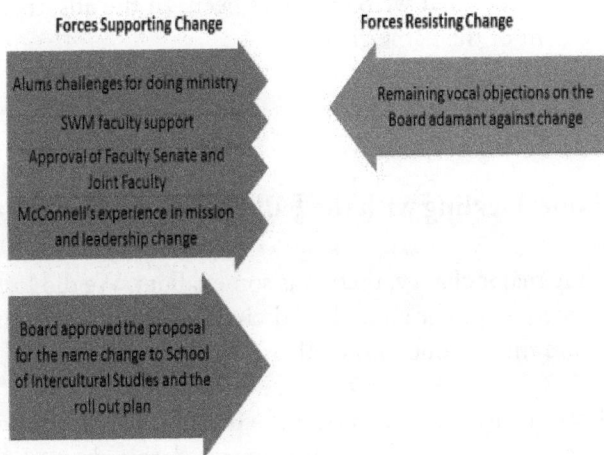

Forces Supporting Change

Forces Resisting Change

Alums challenges for doing ministry

SWM faculty support

Approval of Faculty Senate and Joint Faculty

McConnell's experience in mission and leadership change

Remaining vocal objections on the Board adamant against change

Board approved the proposal for the name change to School of Intercultural Studies and the roll out plan

---

17   Interview with C. Douglas McConnell, June 8, 2015.

18   Internal SIS document, Fall 2003.

message. We were also committed to protecting the safety and well-being of our alumni/ae and their families as they traveled throughout the world. We remain committed to high quality education and training, but making the changes to enable us to do it better in a changing world context. These Talking Points were a way to anchor the change in the historical vision and values of SWM: our name has changed, but we have not; we are now able to do what we have always done and do it better. The other anchor was the celebration of McConnell's installation in Fall 2003. All these took into account the importance of the Symbolic Frame as an important way to stabilize the new name and minimize possible damaging fall out.

Of the four major constituents that had been identified, contacting the students was probably the easiest. They had been part of on-campus discussions and caught the significance of the new name for their futures in spreading the Gospel message. At this time the dean also sent letters to all alumni/ae and donors. Over the Fall of 2003 and Winter 2004, McConnell spent a lot of time on the phone, in lunches, and other meetings with key donors. Pierson's support for the name change was critical in these conversations as many of the donors had been recruited under his deanship and his connections.[19]

The name change was announced in major publications like *Missiology* and *EMQ* with only subtle changes in the ads, emphasizing that we were the same Fuller school that we had always been. In the ads, there was no big announcement of the name change.

Step Four: Dealing with the Fall Out of the New Name

As with any major change, there was some fallout. We did lose donors, and did lose one pledge for an endowed chair, though the Seminary was able to recapture this for one of the other schools.

We did see a drop in students, and continue to struggle with this challenge. But other factors have also impacted this drop, such as the greater restrictions on student visas for international students including the increased requirements for financial guarantees, and the general economic

---

19   Interview with McConnell, June 8, 2015.

downturns that have impacted graduate schools in general. Thus we cannot contribute all of the downturn in enrollment to the name change, though at least part of it was expected.

One of the more fun challenges was what would we be called on campus. School of World Mission had been shortened to SWM, pronounced "swim." But the acronym of School of Intercultural Studies was to be SIS and we did not want to be called "sis." The School of Theology was S O T not "sot," and the School of Psychology was S O P not "sop." So when anyone from the other schools tried to call us "sis" we would respond, politely that we were S I S, unless of course they wanted to be called sop or sot. It worked, and very few people try to call us "sis" anymore!

Reflection on the Four Frames

As a reflection on the change process, I have found it valuable to reflect on each of the four frames from Bolman and Deal and how they can provide insights into the change process.

From the perspective of the Structural, SWM was the smallest of the schools with ongoing tensions and marginalization from the School of Theology. This left SWM, as McConnell described it, in an unprotected relationship with the Seminary as a whole. Thus we carried the full responsibility for navigating the name change process and bearing the burden of any fallout.[20] As an encouraging note, this relationship between the two schools has changed dramatically over the past 10-15 years to where there is a significant increase in both respect and cooperation between the schools. The name change may have played an indirect part in this transformation, but not directly.

From the perspective of the Human Resource frame, SIS has been better able to protect our graduates. In addition to the name change on the web page, degrees are now in line with the new name: Master of Arts in Intercultural Studies, PhD in Intercultural Studies. The Doctor of Missiology has the alternate nomenclature of Doctor of Intercultural Studies which students may choose at the time they submit forms for graduation. In addition Students may petition for a diploma and transcript that reads Fuller Graduate Schools, School of Intercultural Studies, rather

---

20   Interview with Doug McConnell, June 8, 2015

than Fuller Theological Seminary. While this is a DBA alternative, it has proved helpful for some graduates where their lives or ministries are potentially in danger.

The Political frame is the most important to consider in this change process. McConnell worked to clearly identify the various factors and constituencies for and against the name change, and then developing and clearly articulating the arguments that addressed their interests and concerns. The political coalitions on the Board of Trustees were important forces to address directly and to persuade regarding the importance of the name change. Ultimately, their votes were critical and they were the ultimate decision makers in the process. If McConnell had not navigated the challenges of gathering support in a conscientious and careful manner, the name change could have gotten stalled and permanently tabled by the Board. The Political frame also provided insights for creating the Talking Points, and interacting with donors, mission agencies, and the public on the name change.

The Symbolic frame was equally important both in the navigation of the name change through the Board of Trustees, and also in the rollout to the various constituencies. Anchoring the name change in SWM history, values, and purpose were essential to the positive reception of the new name. Given the ongoing fallout of the 9/11 attacks and the renewed interest in reaching the Muslim world with the Gospel message, students and graduates were able to grasp the importance of the new name.

Lessons Learned from This Name Change Process

In my conversation with McConnell, he identified several key lessons that we learned from this name change process:

1. Don't underestimate the power of a negative voice on a committee, as in the strong, vocal opposition on the Board.

2. Likewise, the power of a significant ally and mentor on the Board of Trustees was invaluable.

3. We would have done well to publicize the name change more broadly through articles in journals, and newspapers that explained the process we had gone through to arrive at the new name and the ongoing commitment to the same mission of the school. This is a place where the current Marketing Department has proved helpful.

4. Having the right person to lead the change process was important. Lingenfelter, as both Provost and acting Dean was not in a place to be able to devote the necessary time and effort to navigate the change. McConnell because of his background as a mission leader and having studied in leadership change was the right person at the right time to be able to devote energy and leadership to the entire process. Ultimately it took a team of players to reach the final decision.

While there are still occasional voices that continue to question the wisdom of the name change from School of World Mission to School of Intercultural studies, over ten years later everyone has accepted the new name and are now looking at other changes we need to navigate. "The only constant in life is change."

Tension Between "Roman" And "Catholic" In Catholic Missiology

And Why It Matters

WILLIAM R. BURROWS

DOI: 10.7252/Paper. 000049

About the Author

William R. ("Bill") Burrows, Ph.D., is Research Professor of Missiology in The Center for World Christianity at the New York Theological Seminary. Bill's lifelong scholarly interest has centered on the adaptation of Christianity in non-Western environments and on Christian relations with persons in other faith traditions, particularly on how Christian mission should be understood and carried on in an ecumenical age. He is also Managing Editor Emeritus of Orbis Books.

Introduction

The news in these very days about Pope Francis's encyclical about humanity and the environmental crisis offers a good occasion to illustrate what is at stake in the topic I chose to talk on several months ago. Praise and criticisms have been abundant, but few on either side of the argument show a very deep understanding of *why* a pope would write such a document, nor for the way in which Francis documents his thought in a large-scale hermeneutic of Scripture and in things said by his predecessors. The directness and the marshalling of scientific evidence for the case he makes is new. But he feels compelled to root the seeming novelty in Roman Catholic Tradition. In doing so, he shows that he is not a freelancer nor benevolent dictator. Indeed his way of proceeding is vintage "Roman" in its innate conservatism, and the way he proceeds shows the way in which he feels compelled to be "Catholic" – which is to say, speaks to the whole world, on the one hand, and is anchoring himself in the spirit of the whole Christ, not just in a sectarian enthusiasm for an aspect of Jesus' life, work, and teaching.

Francis stands in a long line of popes who have been critical of the modern project. In particular, since the Enlightenment popes have been exercising their teaching office in two fundamental ways. First, to articulate the Roman Catholic vision of the human community as organic, a living body that is interdependent and must not forget the least. Second, to counteract what they viewed as the negative effects of the Enlightenment. At the risk of glossing over negative elements in the popes' statements and actions, what is enduring in their agenda can be summarized in two points:

1. They viewed modernity's move to democratization as carrying with it the risk that laws and traditions would be treated as solely up to majorities to define – without reference (a) to the law of nature and (b) divine revelation.

2. They sought to counteract the diminishment of revelation – both as contained in Scripture and clarified in Tradition.

Pope Benedict XVI crystallized this position in his well-known phrase, "dictatorship of relativism." He tried to emphasize his belief that the Enlightenment had produced many wonderful things, but those whom we label liberals or progressives seemed never to hear them, just as he had a tin ear for their fear that he and John Paul II wanted to bring humanity back to the bad old days of Pope Pius IX's *Syllabus of Errors* and Vatican Council I's teaching on the infallibility of the pope.[1] Perhaps most of all neither John Paul II nor Benedict seem to have grasped what the Jesuit historian John W. O'Malley called the most important element of the Second Vatican Council:

> … a new way of speaking and behaving [that] … entails a shift in value-system.

> New way of speaking? The implications are profound. To learn a new language so as genuinely to live within it entails an inner transformation. Much more is at stake than learning new words for old concepts. To properly learn a new language means to enter fully into the values and sensibilities of a culture different from one's own and to appropriate them. One gestures, shrugs, bears oneself differently, and responds differently to situations to the point of, to some extent, becoming another person.[2]

---

1   For the full text of the *Syllabus*, see Henricus Denzinger and Adolphus Schönmetzer, eds., *Enchiridion Symbolorum* (Rome: Herder, 36th ed., 1976), pp. 576-84, §§ 2901-80; for an abridged English version, see Jacques Dupuis, ed., *The Christian Faith in the Doctrinal Documents of the Catholic Church* (Staten Island, NY: Alba House, 7th ed., 2001), pp. 37-42; see also Dupuis, pp. 42-51 for Vatican Council I's articulation of the doctrine of revelation, faith, and faith and reason; see also pp. 316-22 on the papacy and papal infallibility; see also *Dei Verbum* (Vatican II "Decree on Revelation," 1965), §§ 7-10 for a balanced view on the interrelationship of Scripture and Tradition. This section, arguably one of the most important in the documents of the Council, concludes with the words, "It is clear, therefore, that in the supremely wise arrangement of God, sacred Tradition, sacred Scripture, and the Magisterium of the Church are so connected and associated that one of them cannot stand without the other. Working together, each in its own way under the action of the one Holy Spirit, they all contribute effectively to the salvation of souls."

2   John W O'Malley, *What Happened at Vatican II?* (Cambridge: Harvard University Press), p. 50.

Anyone who has struggled with learning a new language and culture knows that what O'Malley says is true. The reality is dramatically portrayed in the words of Andrew Walls: "The fundamental missionary experience is to live on terms set by others."[3]

The question I address does not presume that I think Catholic conservatives, who insist on close readings of Vatican II, are malevolent; indeed, I want to state clearly that I appreciate the indispensable role of conservatives in "conserving" at the same time as I bring into relief the tension between aspirations to be both "Roman" and "Catholic" in ecclesiology and missiology. The positive side of the way Roman Catholicism works is expressed well by Lamin Sanneh when he says:

> Catholicism's doctrinal core is arguably more stable than that of many other variants of Christianity. Even if its directives are contested, the church's magisterium is recognized for what it is. The catechism and the instrument of papal encyclicals together have defined Catholic faith just as that faith is enshrined in the church's liturgical life, with Jesus Christ at its core. Against the cultural fragmentation of modern life, that is a considerable advantage. Catholics may crack wise at this heritage and from the flanks even nibble away at it, but it's hard to dismiss it as of no value.[4]

On a more personal note, he adds,

> For me Catholicism became an exit strategy from the confinement of upscale liberal agnosticism that has long commanded the world of academia. I felt a lively sense of emancipation surrounded by the signs and symbols of the mystery of God in the ungrudging, faithful witness of the church. That fact was the connection to the worldwide community of faith spread within and across national boundaries. It relieved me of the double burden of having to face wearying interrogation by other Christians, and of

---

3   Andrew F Walls, *The Cross-Cultural Process in Christian History: Studies in the Transmission and Appropriation of Faith* (Maryknoll, NY: Orbis Books, 2002), p. 41.

4   Lamin Sanneh, *Summoned from the Margin: Homecoming of an African* (Grand Rapids, MI: Eerdmans, 2012), p. 259.

the defensiveness it begs. I could identify myself with other Catholics without having to work the levers of citizenship, race, language, education, taste, class, sex, or education. My privileged position in an elite university accustomed to thinking of itself as entitled to due deference ceased to determine my religious standing.[5]

The positive side of "Roman" Catholicism is, I would argue, expressed concisely here. Rome proceeds slowly and is often behind the times, but it does so in a world quickly moving from fad to fad and vogue to vogue. With a nod to Alexander Pope, being not the first by whom the new are tried nor the last to lay the old aside is not all bad, as long as one is merely keeping antiquarians happy.

In what follows, I will be referring to the work of other scholars, but much of what follows will be, in the words of the scholastic theology on which I was weaned, "speculative." The rules of scholarship require careful documentation of what one says or writes, but at the age of 72 and after spending half my adult life preparing for or taking part in the missionary apostolates of the Society of the Divine Word and the other half in the employ of the Catholic Foreign Mission Society of America (better known as "Maryknoll") as part of the team that publishes Orbis Books, there are things I have picked up that I can't document carefully. I will not apologize for that.

In that vein, it was with a sigh of relief that I started reading recently a book sent to me by my friend Paul Gifford, a noted sociologist, historian, and analyst of Sub-Saharan Africa, like me a former priest who has both a clerical insider's and a lay outsider's view of things Catholic. Paul has a quality that is rare in scholars. He ruminates over the meaning of inconvenient facts that call into question the sort of consensus that explains too much with too little backing.

What I like about Paul's writing is something I hope you will find in what follows. Quoting Keith Thomas, Gifford notes that in certain areas of knowledge one will not find "knock-down evidence of statistics, but the wholly justified implication ... that these matters are best understood with the aid of what German social scientists and theorists call the faculty of

---

5   Sanneh, *Homecoming*, p. 267.

Verstehung.[6] *Verstehen* ("to understand") and *Verstehung* ("understanding") in their deepest sense are often the products of Eureka moments that lead to paradigm shifts à la Thomas Kuhn[7] -- if one has waded through the evidence and reaches insights that (1) answer the relevant questions on the matters being studied and (2) better explain what is happening than regnant constructs. Achieving insight is rather a lot more than producing mere bright ideas.

Alfred North Whitehead once observed that speculation on a grand scale "is superficially sceptical … but it obtains its urge from a deep ultimate faith that the nature of things is penetrable by reason." Scholarship, on the other hand, as Whitehead observes, "is superficially conservative of belief. But its tone of mind leans towards a fundamental negation."[8] In our discussion of the tension between "Roman" and Catholic" in mission study and practice, I will be speculating on things that go beyond what scholarship can "prove" or "document." Much of what follows will not be " 'conclusive' in any hard sense," but, because like Paul Gifford, "I think they are revealing of the reality I am describing, and my reason for thinking so is my 30 years of exposure and experience."[9]

To be clear, I think it is important for Roman Catholics to be both Roman and Catholic, and that the tendency to scorn the Roman is dangerous. At least as dangerous as the tendency to be slavishly subservient to it. Clearly Pope Benedict XVI had this in view in his insistence that "faith itself is cultural" and does not exist in some "naked state, as sheer religion."[10] And he goes on to note,

---

6   Paul Gifford, *Christianity, Development and Modernity in Africa* (London: Hurst & Company, 2015), p. 7.

7   Thomas S. Kuhn, *The Structure of Scientific Revolutions,* 2nd ed.) Chicago: University of Chicago Press, 1970).

8   Alfred North Whitehead, *Adventure of Ideas* (New York: Macmillan, 1933), p. 137.

9   Gifford, *Christianity in Africa*, p.7

10   Joseph Ratzinger *Truth and Tolerance: Christian Belief and the World Religions* (San Francisco: Ignatius Press, 2004), p. 67.

Anyone entering the Church has to be aware that he is entering a separate, active cultural entity with her own many-layered intercultural character that has grown up in the course of history. Without a certain exodus, a breaking off with one's life in all its aspects, one cannot become a Christian ... We cannot repeat the Incarnation at will, in the sense of repeatedly taking Christ's flesh away from him, so to speak, and offering him some other flesh instead ... Christ remains the same, even according to his body. But he is drawing us to him."[11]

For Ratzinger, this is why Christianity is at war with relativism. Christ is the same now as he was at the Resurrection, and being a Christian means entering into fellowship with a people journeying through history in union with this Christ.

The Central Issue

I have said that I want to explore the topic of the tension in Roman Catholic attitudes toward mission between being "Catholic," on the one hand, and "Roman," on the other. Both adjectives throw light on and cast shadows over our conception of the mission of the church. Note that both "Roman" and "Catholic" are important as adjectives modifying the noun "church." And because to say "church" is to speak of "mission," it is important to see the vital importance of understanding the tension between them in the light of Roman Catholic history and the historical situation of globalized Christianity. This globalized situation, I wish to suggest, challenges us – Catholics, Orthodox, Ecumenical Protestants, Evangelical denominational and non-denominational Protestants, Anabaptists, Pentecostals, and Charismatics – to seek a form of Christian unity and self-understanding in which both the universal and the "local" – the latter in analogy to the way "Roman" functions in Roman Catholicism – are vitally integrated in respectful love and, yes, requisite tension.

Why? Briefly said, because the balance has shifted so far in the direction "local" and "contextual" Christianity over against biblical claims of the "universality" and "finality" of Jesus the Christ, that the task of Christians

11   Ratzinger, *Truth and Tolerance*, p. 71.

becoming ever more deeply the body of Christ is imperative. Because I believe that the proclamation of the decisive role and person of Jesus as Christ in the revelation of God's nature and purposes for the cosmos and humanity is, as Pope St John Paul II calls it, the "permanent priority of mission"[12]; and therefore we badly need to understand the centrality of "the church" in ensuring that Jesus, the Christ/Messiah is not occluded and that Jacques Dupuis's "Christocentric Trinitarianism" is maintained.[13]

Genuine Christianity is not "Christomonistic," for the Father, the Son, and the Holy Spirit are each and together essential in the mystery of salvation. That said, to follow Jesus entails a way of life that is *Christomorphic*, which is to say the paschal mystery shapes (*morphóō*) Christian identity, practice and belief.[14] It is also a vision in which the challenge of First Corinthians 3:9 as "God's servants, working together" must be taken very seriously.

And lest you think the words "the centrality of the church" above were mere filler, the subtext of everything that follows is a question asked by Graymoor Friar James Puglisi when he or his editors at Eerdmans put the following title on a recent book: *How can the Petrine Ministry Be a Service to the Unity of the Universal Church?*[15] If one is to follow the Acts of the Apostles, Peter's ministry moved from Jerusalem to Antioch to Rome.

---

12 Pope St John Paul II, Encyclical Letter, *Redemptoris Missio*, ("On the Permanent Validity of the Church's Missionary Mandate" [Rome: Libreria Editrice Vaticana, 1990]), § 44.

13 Jacques Dupuis, *Christianity and the Religions: From Confrontation to Dialogue* (Maryknoll, NY: Orbis Books), pp. 87-95, where Dupuis makes the case for Christian theocentrism being a Christocentric Trinitarianism, not a form of low Christology that, in effect, makes Christ a teacher in the way John Hick's and Paul Knitter's theocentrism and soteriocentrism do.

14 See Galatians 4:19, " ... until Christ is formed (*morphôthê*) in you." I find Richard R Niebuhr magisterial on the subject of Christomorphism; see his *Schleiermacher on Christ and Religion: A New Introduction* (New York: Scribners, 1964), pp. 210-59.

15 (Grand Rapids: Eerdmans, 2010). Fr Puglisi is a former superior general of the Graymoor Friars, a Catholic order in the Franciscan tradition with roots in Anglicanism, one of whose principle apostolates is the promotion of Christian unity.

As both John O'Malley[16] and Eamon Duffy[17] note in their histories of the papacy, however, the development of the papal office is not a simple, straightforward matter, nor is the office of bishop as attributed to Peter exercised in the same way as it would be in later years. But the consensus of historians is that Peter did reside in and lead a community in Rome and by the second century, that tradition was the basis for a recognition of Roman primacy in much of the then-infant *ecclesia* scattered throughout the world.

An Etymological and Historical Detour

The etymology of the name "Roman Catholic Church" is anomalous in that the two adjectives are in contradiction with one another. *Roman* refers to a particular place. *Catholic* denotes something universal. Grasping the dialectic tension between the two words is important if one is to understand how the church that claims half the world's Christians as members understands itself.

"Catholic," we are usually told, comes from the Greek word *katholikos* (universal) and has an "extensive" or "geographic" meaning. At a deeper level, however, lie the words *kata* ("according to") and *holon* ("whole"). *Kata* is most familiar to readers of the New Testament as the preposition used to name a version of the story of Jesus, a "gospel" (*euaggelion*), as in the phrase "the Gospel 'according to' Luke" (*kata loukon*).

The elided version of the two words *kat'olon* also has a theological or intensive meaning that needs more emphasis than it usually gets. By *intensive* I indicate that what is connoted is "according to the whole [i.e., gospel or Christ]." That gospel is "catholic," not sectarian. It connotes in other words, the Christ revealed in the full dimensions of New Testament and Apostolic age teaching. We are more familiar with the extensive sense of the words where "the catholic church" is the term favored for speaking of the universal church spread from Lyons to Bagdad, from Jerusalem

16 John W O'Malley, *A History of the Popes: From Peter to the Present* (New York: Rowman & Littlefield, 2010), pp. 13-21 (Chapter 2, "After Peter and Paul").

17 Eamon Duffy, *Saints and Sinners: A History of the Popes* (New Haven: Yale University Press, 1997), pp 1-36.

and Alexandria to Rome and down into Ethiopia. The second – what I am calling "the intensive sense" of the word – denotes a local church recognized by other churches in the nascent communion of churches as one that preserved the whole gospel as the message *of* Jesus about God's Promise and Kingdom, but also *about* Jesus as the Christ, the universal savior.

The overseers (*episkopoi*, bishops) of the principal churches did this by judging that catholicity and three other key characteristics of a genuine church were present ("unity" [with the universal church], "holiness," and "apostolicity") in a local church (primarily understood a local community or nexus of communities led by a bishop). In acting this way, they were considered to be exercising authority as legitimate successors of the Twelve (apostles), declaring congregations to be genuine assemblies (Greek, *ekklesiē*, plural of *ekklesia*, whence the Latin word for "church," *ecclesia*) of God's new people in Christ. A local community was recognized as part of the universal church only insofar as it was *intensively* catholic, which is to say that *a church was judged to be one wherein the whole Christ was present, his paschal mystery was liturgically celebrated, and the whole gospel was taught and lived.*

The Riddle and Ambiguity of Roman Primacy

In this context, as its self-understanding developed, the "Roman" catholic church, although it was but one of the five major patriarchal churches, from very early on claimed: (1) to have been founded by the apostles Peter and Paul; (2) that Peter was its first bishop; (3) that Peter had been given primacy over the other members of the Twelve by Christ; and (4) that his successors continued to enjoy that primacy. Over time, this primacy came to be understood as entailing the Bishop of Rome's divinely conferred ministry to symbolize and effect the unity of the universal church (*ecclesia catholica*).

In making this claim in ongoing centuries, the church of Rome invoked words such as the following from Irenaeus of Lyons (c. 130–200), in his work *Against Heresies* (Book III, Chapter 3). Irenaeus argues that anyone can see the evidence for the lineage from Peter to the present Bishop of Rome. Moreover, he says, the tradition that the church of Rome is "universally known" to have been "founded and organized at Rome by the two most glorious apostles, Peter and Paul"; and he maintains that "it is a matter of necessity that every church should agree with this church on account of its pre-eminent authority." In addition, the memory of early bishops such as Polycarp (c. 69–155, whose testimony on the centrality of Rome is recounted by Irenaeus) were invoked as proofs of Rome's preeminence from earliest times.

The point here is not that the case for what the Roman Catholic church *now claims* was clinched in a way convincing to all *today*, but that belief in its primacy was important both to other churches and to the Roman church's self-understanding. That Roman primacy entails "jurisdiction" – the power to command obedience to its dictates – over all other churches is hotly disputed, both by Catholics and others. And here we are talking about the ambiguity of these claims.[18]

Imagining that fourth century Catholicism represents some sort of falling away from an a-political, religiously pristine status that existed before Constantine is an oversimplification. Equally simplistic are claims that late medieval, early modern reform movements started beyond the Alps leap-frogged over twelve centuries of Roman decadence to re-create the true church. I don't mean that there was no decadence. Anyone who reads the history of the Medici family knows better. But the reality is much more complex than mere corruption. The barbarians had pressured the Romans even before Constantine, and the sack of Rome in 410 was less a uniquely cataclysmic event, than the natural outcome of a centuries-long march of "barbarian" nations coming off the Russian Steppes.[19] As the Western Roman Empire declined and fell in the fifth and sixth centuries and as pressure from the Germanic nations brought about an entirely new

---

18   In these matters Brian Tierney's *The Origins of Papal Infallibility 1150-1350: A Study on the Concepts of Infallibility, Sovereignty, and Tradition in the Middle Ages* (Leiden: Brill, 1972), pp. 22-31, remains magisterial. Tierney shows how the Decretists of the reform movements of the 12th and 13th centuries never saw papal power as having the capacity of a pope to alter "permanent truths of Scriptural revelation." For them (the Decretists) "the pope was a supreme ruler within the framework of divine revelation established by Scripture, not an absolute monarch set above it" (p. 30). To complete the picture, see Brian Tierney, *The Crisis of Church and State 1050-1300* (Englewood Cliffs, NJ: Prentice-Hall, 1964).

19   See Peter Heather, *Empires and Barbarians: The Fall of Rome and the Birth of Europe* (Oxford: Oxford University Press, 2009), pp. 151-206, Chapter 4, "Migration and Frontier Collapse." Equally interesting is Allesandro Barbert, tr. Allan Cameron, *Charlemagne: Father of a Continent* (London: The Folio Society, 2006). What both books show is the immense complexity of the organization

social-political reality, bishops of Rome assumed the mantle of guarantors of both civil and ecclesial order. While *Roman* evoked a specific locality in the semantic world of the age, it also recalled a crumbling world's memory of universal order, the *pax Romana*. The key to what Roman "Catholicism" *meant* in the medieval period stems, then, from that local (Roman) church's role in articulating what was thought to be the proper apostolic order of the universal (catholic) church in vastly new circumstances. In the West, the crumbling structures of the Roman Empire were taken over by the church. Peoples hungering for order were, for the most part, glad to accept it. Viewed from the perspective of an Anglican and Edwardian gentleman, the brother of a missionary bishop in India, however, the post-Reformation world was less impressed with the medieval synthesis. Listen again to Alfred North Whitehead:

> When the Western world accepted Christianity, Caesar conquered; and the received text of Western theology was edited by his lawyers. The code of Justinian and the theology of Justinian are two volumes expressing one movement of the human spirit. The brief Galilean vision of humility flickered throughout the ages certainly … But the deeper idolatry of fashioning God in the image of the Egyptian, Persian, and Roman imperial rulers was retained. The Church gave unto God the attributes which belonged exclusively to Caesar.[20]

Rise of Islam, Divorce of Eastern and Western Christianity

As the Empire split between the Latin West and the Greek East, the division of European and West Asian Catholic Christianity into complimentary and mutually recognizing forms of Catholicism was solidified. What is often forgotten is that after the rise of Islam in 622, the Catholic, Orthodox churches of the East — the Oriental Orthodox, Coptic, Syrian, Armenian, Ethiopian, and Indian — declined and were forgotten by the Western Church. The Greek and Latin Catholic churches

---

of Catholic Europe in the aftermath of Rome's collapse. Rather than a disaster of turning from "genuine" or "primitive" Christianity, the post-Constantinian world was a remarkable achievement.

20 Alfred North Whitehead, *Process and Reality: An Essay in Cosmology*, Gifford Lectures, Edinburgh, 1927-28 (New York: Macmillan, 1929), pp. 519-20.

went their distinct but cousinly ways until 1054, when they split at just about the time Slavic Catholic Orthodoxy was growing in significance as a result of the missionary labors of Cyril, Methodius, and their successors. And Roman Catholics must admit that the split was to a great extent caused by the arrogant Roman exercise and inflation of its primacy.

For our purposes, what is important is twofold. There was a time when a variety of churches — Greek and Latin churches, as well as Oriental Orthodox churches of the East — recognized each other as "catholic" in every essential way. They argued about the adequacy of doctrines propagated at councils such as Chalcedon (454), but they were led by bishops in communion with the major patriarchal sees, bishops believed to have authority conferred on them by apostolic succession and the will of God. In addition, with varying emphases and differing liturgical languages and traditions, they were united in a form of worship begun in baptism, centered on the Eucharist, and dedicated to expounding orthodox teaching based in scripture and tradition.

"Roman" Catholicism Develops in the West

It is hard to know whether it is more accurate to see the growth of Christianity in the West as the result of a missionary movement or as a form of religio-cultural diffusion aided by Merovingian and Carolingian kings and emperors. It suffices here to recognize that the growth of Celtic Christianity in Brittany, Wales, and Ireland and its expansion into northern Britain and eventually into northern Europe through the work of such legendary figures as Patrick (mid to late fifth century), Columba (c. 521–597), and monks sent by Pope Gregory I ("the Great," c. 540–604) began a process wherein Roman liturgy, canons, and usages eventually became ascendant. Owing in large part to the rise of monasteries following the rule of the Italian Saint Benedict of Nursia (c. 480–550), the Catholicism of the church north of the Alps would be Roman in flavor and look to Rome for guidance when theological and ecclesial matters were in dispute or kings and princes were trampling on church prerogatives. In addition to spurring the diffusion of Christianity northward, Gregory took a strong hand in ruling the church of Italy, upholding and broadening the recognition and power of the See of Rome. Unfortunately, he did so in ways that often alienated churches that took their signals from the Patriarch of Constantinople, whose claim to be the "Ecumenical Patriarch" Gregory refused to recognize. In the East, accordingly, recognition of Roman primacy was understood to grant Rome a primacy of honor, not authority to decide matters in dispute in other churches. When Rome insisted that primacy entailed the authority of jurisdiction, a split that had been long in the making occurred.

The development of what becomes the Roman Catholic Church that is still recognizable today came in a centuries-long process too seldom identified. In it, migrating Teutonic and other tribes effectively "Germanized" Latin Catholicism. (In using the word *German*, I am speaking of not only the Goths, Franks, Saxons, and Vandals, but also, although loosely, of the Vikings and original Britons.) Between the beginnings of the migration of the Germanic nations until relative stability was attained in about 678, the Germans were coming to terms with Roman culture. They admired its laws, architecture, methods of building roads, fortresses, and houses, while they resisted other elements. In terms of faith, some Germanic peoples became acquainted with Arian constructions of Christian identity, others with the Catholic and Celtic emissaries. No matter what kind of contacts, all had to work through the ways in which traditional Germanic warrior honor cultures would adapt to new conditions and whether and how they would take on the new religion.

The societies into which Latin Christianity was grafted were ones in which religion and politics were closely aligned. Religion was predominantly magical, in contradistinction, as Russell says, "to being a pre-dominantly doctrinal and ethical" reality. In addition, the German view of politics was marked by a form of "sacral kingship," a worldview that will loom large in coming battles over the relative powers of princes and bishops.[21]

In the end, the Roman form of Catholicism symbolized by St. Wilfrid, bishop of York (634–709) triumphed over Celtic usages in Britain at the Synod of Whitby (664) and was brought to the continent by St. Boniface (c. 675–754), who was a Benedictine and loyal to the papacy. That allegiance, while not without strains, would become normative north of the Alps, but the process was not straightforward, and the ratio of Germanic to

---

21 See James C. Russell, *The Germanization of Early Medieval Catholicism: A Socio-Historical Approach to Religious Transformation* (New York and Oxford: Oxford University Press, 1994), part 2, pp. 107-214. For a fascinating example of the ways in which Christian doctrine developed under the umbrella of the history analyzed by Russell, see Peter Brown, *The Ransom of the Soul: Afterlife and Wealth in Early Western Christianity* (Cambridge: Harvard University Press, 2015), chapter 4, "Penance and the Other World in Gaul," pp. 115-47.

Mediterranean-Roman elements was negotiated over several centuries. As the Holy Roman Empire took shape in the north with the coronation of Otto I in 962 and conquered the northern two-thirds of Italy by 1100, one can fairly speak of the "Germanization" of Roman Catholicism. This takes place precisely in the age when canon lawyers are systematizing church law and bringing forth theories that the Pope has, by divine will, universal jurisdiction (the power to emanate laws that must be obeyed by all a ruler's subjects). This sets the scene for the medieval struggle among bishops, princes, kings, emperors, and popes over where the jurisdiction of bishops and popes begins and ends.

What is central to this Germanized Roman Catholicism? First, devotions to saints and a sense of the closeness of the dead took an important place; the Germanic world was the dwelling place of various kinds of "presences" and non-human agencies; and any religion worth adopting, had to adapt to that reality. Shrines associated with saints, where miracles were performed, grew up, at least partly to provide heroes to replace those of ancient Norse and German sagas. Pilgrimages to holy places dedicated to the saints and God's mother were important; these saints were said to be more powerful than the old nature, place, and ancestral spirits. Rituals associated with the saints, in addition, took the place of pagan rites.

Significantly, the liturgy of the Mass and the monastic liturgy of the hours were developed and became central to the official cult of the church. Amidst all the varieties of devotion that replaced the old magic, the rhythm of the liturgical year celebrated according to proscribed liturgical texts was designed to keep the various devotions and pilgrimages subservient to the Christ of the creeds. The Mass was where God's grace and power were met; though to be sure that sins were *really* forgiven, indulgences and sacramentals were sold and blessed so the faithful could be assured that the fruits of Christ's sacrifice would reach them.

Germanized-Roman Catholicism, in other words, had been born. And onto the root of cultural conversion of Christianity from Hebrew to Hellenistic outlooks begun by Paul and carried forward by Greek-speaking Apostolic and post-Apostolic Fathers, which were adapted to the Latin mindset by Tertullian, Cyprian, and Augustine, was grafted the Germanic vine.

Reality was messy, of course, and in areas like paying for indulgences, popular piety and greedy clerics' need for money for their projects overwhelmed orthodoxy, so much so that by the 13th century many of the themes of 16th century reformers had been foreshadowed. The Franciscan and Dominican orders were founded and became the agents of reform.

The Splintering of Western Christendom And the Crisis of Our Age

We all know the basics of the history of the Reformation, and I do not intend to recite that history. My basic point is that Catholic reforms under St Francis and St Dominic antedated the Reformation and proceeded under the inspiration of Catholic impulses. The conversion of St Ignatius of Loyola and the creation both of his *Spiritual Exercises* and the order he founded were not intended primarily to combat Protestants.[22] Yet many of the goals of these saints were shared with the great Reformers: Hus, Zwingli, Calvin, Luther, and Simons. I speak, of course, of the debt Protestantism owes to the early modern impulses that we call collectively the Renaissance. The Jesuit historian John O'Malley is magisterial on that point. I commend his work to you, especially his little book *Trent and All That*.[23]

It is clear, nevertheless, that the renewal of Catholicism would not have occurred without the upheaval caused by the Lutheran and the Reformed movements of the sixteenth century. An Erasmus may have been more learned and enjoy a much more pleasant temperament than his contemporaries in Wittenberg and Geneva, but he would never have sparked the movement needed to cleanse Catholic Christendom. Luther and Calvin returned to the Scriptures and found in them little to no basis for the Roman Catholicism of their day. By luck or through providence, their revolution coincided with revolutions in scholarship, the growth of national self-awareness, and resentment of clerical domination.

---

22   See John W O'Malley, *The First Jesuits* (Cambridge: Harvard University Press, 1993), pp. 284-328.

23   John W O'Malley, *Trent and All That: Renaming Catholicism in the Early Modern Era* (Cambridge: Harvard University Press, 2000).

If one takes a look at some of the greatest missionaries of the early modern era, and especially if one reads their letters, it becomes clear that Catholic reforms were producing results, too. Jesuits such as Francis Xavier, Alessandro Valignano, Ippolito Desideri, Roberto De Nobili, Matteo Ricci, Alexandre de Rhodes, and José de Acosta; the Dominican Bartholomé de las Casas; and the Franciscans Junípero Serra and his friend and biographer Francisco Palóu did not come from a decadent church. To Jesuits active in Asia in the 16th through the 18th centuries goes the *palme d'oro* for grasping the depths of the interreligious and intercultural problems Christianity faced in civilizations whose elites at least had undergone what the German philosopher of history Karl Jaspers would call the axial period. By that term he meant undergoing a process in which "Human existence becomes the object of meditation, *as history*" when human beings "feel and know something extraordinary is beginning in their own present."[24]

Catholic missionaries of the 16th through the 18th centuries, when Protestant missions from the West begin in earnest, struggled with the question of cultural adaptation, and not always successfully. Spanish and Portuguese missionaries in South America, Mexico, and "New" Mexico (today's Texas, Arizona, California, and New Mexico) in particular were seen by the crown and saw themselves as agents of Iberian imperialism. That many of the missionaries judged the behavior of colonial administrators, the military, and colonizers to violate the rights of the Indians does not change the fact that they also saw themselves as an integral part of a work in which they were preparing Indians to be useful citizens in an imperial-colonial project. The salaries of the missionaries were paid by the colonial government under the aegis of the *patronato real*. And to read the life of Junípero Serra in a recent book that has taken advantage of deep research into archives in California, Mexico, and Spain is to be shocked at the Franciscans' self-identification as missionaries sponsored by the king and dedicated to extending his kingdom.

> As a Catholic missionary and loyal Spaniard, Serra never doubted for an instant that his worldview was objectively superior to the indigenous worldviews. But this trip helped him begin to grasp that an effective missionary strategy would have to acknowledge the existence of the

---

24   Karl Jaspers, *The Origin and Goal of History*, trans. Michael Bullock (London: Routledge & Kegan Paul, 1953), p. 5.

spaces between the various cultures. A successful strategy would have to be tentative and provisional, and its results would be gradual.[25]

And in another place:

> The colonial government that established the missions intended for them to be temporary institutions. The Indians were to learn the Spanish religion, language, and way of life, and then after a period of ten years or so, the church was to be turned into a regular parish (a process known as "secularization"). The mission lands were to be divided among the Indians, who would then take their places in society as Spanish and Catholic farmers and ranchers.[26]

Drawing Conclusions

It seems to me that our missionary moment today requires a Christian movement that is both extensively and intensively catholic, one that is marked also by holiness, unity, and apostolicity. The four belong together, for they are intrinsically related to the dynamic of following Christ in our globalizing world as when the Christian movement center moved from Jerusalem to Asia Minor and finally to Rome in a series of events recounted in Acts 10-16, one of the key parts of which consists in the words of Peter:

> And God who knows the human heart testified to them by giving them the Holy Spirit, just as he did to us; and in cleansing their hearts by faith he has made no distinction between them and us. Now therefore why are you putting God to the test by placing on the neck of the disciples a yoke that neither our ancestors nor we have been able to

---

25 Rose Marie Beebe and Robert M Senkewicz, *Junípero Serra: California, Indians, and the Transformation of a Missionary* (Norman, OK: University of Oklahoma Press, 2015), Kindle Edition, loc. 3039.

26 Beebe, *Serra*, Kindle loc. 3844.

bear? On the contrary, we believe that we will be saved through the grace of the Lord Jesus, just as they will (Acts 15:8-11).

Catholics enjoy such texts, for in them they see Peter rising above the church of Jerusalem led by James and making the decision that confers legitimacy on Paul's and Barnabas's mission to the gentiles. Ah, would that history were kind to those who rely on proof-texting when reality is so much more complicated! Catholics certainly have much to repent of in their long history. Indeed, Pope St John Paul II recognized that the institution he embodied, the Roman Papacy, was to many an obstacle to attaining that unity:

> [A]s I acknowledged on the important occasion of a visit to the World Council of Churches in Geneva on 12 June 1984, the Catholic Church's conviction that in the ministry of the Bishop of Rome she has preserved, in fidelity to the Apostolic Tradition and the faith of the Fathers, the visible sign and guarantor of unity, constitutes a difficulty for most other Christians, whose memory is marked by certain painful recollections. To the extent that we are responsible for these, I join my Predecessor Paul VI in asking forgiveness.[27]

Careful study reveals that the legitimacy of the present shape of papal office cannot be called the only legitimate way Roman primacy can be exercised over the Roman Catholic half of the world's Christians. Even more, a notion of primacy that includes the right directly to exercise authority over all churches is a non-starter for the non-Roman half of the world's Christians. It is increasingly under fire even within Roman Catholicism; and much of the enthusiasm for Pope Francis comes from hope that he might seek a new way forward.

Still, the perpetual splintering of the Protestant third of the world's Christians is itself a cautionary tale. And as to the claim that Scripture alone can govern the church, it is self-evident the Scriptures are not self-interpreting. Take the anguish that they are going through today over how to interpret the Bible in both testaments on homosexuality, gender identity, the position of women, and related issues. I read both *The Christian Century* and *Christianity Today* on a regular basis. It is hard to

---

27 Pope St John Paul II, *Ut Unum Sint* (Encyclical Letter on Christian Unity, "That All May Be One" [Rome: Libreria Vaticana, 1995]) § 88.

imagine that they are both respected Protestant "Christian" journals, so little does either segment of Protestantism respect the other. I also read *The National Catholic Reporter*, *America*, and *Commonweal*. The same is true there. The cultural divide among Catholics is deep and the rivers between them are both deep and bitter.

My friend Ed Schroeder introduced me to Luther's sixteenth century recovery of the Pauline doctrine on gospel and law. Indeed, he converted me believing that Luther's retrieval of the Pauline Gospel is a far better interpretation of what Christianity is about than the standard Roman Catholic envisionment of grace perfecting nature. But equally important was Ed's introducing me to the Book of Concord on the *Adiaphora*. Here one finds in paragraph 9 the Lutheran formula for dealing with external matters that do not touch the heart of faith.

> Therefore we believe, teach, and confess that the congregation of God of every place and every time has, according to its circumstances, the good right, power, and authority [in matters truly adiaphora] to change, to diminish, and to increase them, without thoughtlessness and offense, in an orderly and becoming way, as at any time it may be regarded most profitable, most beneficial, and best for [preserving] good order, [maintaining] Christian discipline ... and the edification of the Church.[28]

What is essential is the teaching on Christ, the Gospel as Promise, the forgiveness of sin, and justification through faith. It would be nice if we could put our sexual morality disagreements in the category of *adiaphora* and concentrate solely on preaching the Gospel. Experience, though, shows we cannot manage it.

Why bring this up? Because I think that the traditional Roman way of dealing with such matters has a great deal to commend it. For something on the order of 1,500 years, a nascent and later robust, perhaps too robust, concept of Roman primacy guided Western Christianity toward proclaiming the centrality of Christ and celebrating his mysteries liturgically while allowing exercises in popular piety that served as a bridge to the essentials of faith.

---

28 *Solid Declaration of the Book of Concord,* Article X, para. 9 (accessed at http://bookofconcord.org/sd-adiaphora.php on 25 June 2015)

Is something more evangelical possible in a reformed papacy? In his study of Pope John Paul II's *Ut Unum Sint*, retired Archbishop John Quinn singles out seven elements that the pope himself identifies as key to primatial vigilance and the service of unity. I quote Quinn:

- Vigilance over handing down of the word

- Vigilance over the celebration of the liturgy and the sacraments

- Vigilance over the Church's mission, discipline and the Christian life

- Vigilance over the requirements of the common good of the Church should anyone be tempted to overlook it in the pursuit of personal interests

- The primatial duty to admonish, to caution, and to declare at times that this or that opinion . . . is irreconcilable with the unity of faith

- The primatial duty to speak in the name of all the Pastors in communion with him when circumstances require it

- The primatial duty – under very specific (and limited) conditions to declare *ex cathedra* that a certain doctrine belongs the deposit of faith[29]

My suspicion is that a pope with the personality of Jorge Mario Bergoglio may have a better chance of making such things seem attractive than John Paul. But where John Paul could bring only conservatives, Francis appears to be battling with them in his attempt to simplify the papacy and reduce its elaborate habits. Thus it is well to remember the question that Robert Mickens asked in the 26 May 2015 issue of *The National Catholic Reporter*: "Can Pope Francis succeed in reforming the Curia?"

None of us knows yet the answer to that question, but when I dream of the future, I imagine the zeal and freedom of Protestant associational methods of operating in ad hoc manners combined with both the dynamism and stability of Catholic religious orders. Each order is self-

---

29   John R Quinn, *The Reform of the Papacy: The Costly Call to Christian Unity* (New York: Crossroad, 1999), p. 29.

governing under the umbrella of canon law and the pope as vicar of Peter who – at his best – discerns both how to encourage the auspicious new and to subject mere novelties and self-aggrandizing grand-standing to sober testing … with the love, patience, and wisdom that heals and increases, taking care not to wound.

APM

Conference Papers

Diakonia and Mission: Charting the Ambiguity

DOI: 10.7252/Paper. 000050

About the Author

Benjamin L. Hartley is Associate Professor of Christian Mission and Director of United Methodist Studies at Palmer Theological Seminary, the Seminary of Eastern University, Philadelphia, Pennsylvania. He is an ordained deacon in the Eastern Pennsylvania Conference of the United Methodist Church.

Around the world individual local churches, denominations, seminaries, training institutes, and even governments struggle with the meaning of *diakonia* and its cognates (*diakonein, diakonos,* etc.). In large part the ambiguity of *diakonia* as a Greek term is due to the usage of linguistic variations of the term outside of its New Testament context; *diakonie* in German is best translated as religiously-motivated social work. Scandinavian languages have similar terms with like meaning. *Diakonia* as a New Testament term has been interpreted to mean acts of lowly, humble, service, and this field of meaning has been assumed to apply equally well to what Germans call *diakonie.* The precise nature of *diakonie* as a religious term, however, is contested in the secular cultural context of many European countries. Linguistic research on *diakonia* in the New Testament context by Roman Catholic scholar John N. Collins further challenges the traditional understanding of *diakonia* and *diakonie* as lowly, humble, service. Needless to say, a term translated as "ministry" and "service" in English Bibles directly impinges on our understanding of mission. The ambiguity surrounding *diakonia*, therefore, is germane to challenges in defining mission in general and is also directly relevant to our 2015 APM conference theme of examining the naming of mission program titles.

The word's assumed connotation of "lowly, humble, service" has influenced ecclesial discourse in ways which have not always been positive. The ubiquitous use of "servant leadership" language, for example, as the paramount understanding of ministry can be a problem for a number of reasons which I elaborate on later in this paper. Our APM colleague Bill Burrows pointed out years ago the problem of reductionism in this move away from the rich spiritual depth of ministry – observed perhaps most poignantly in the liturgical theology of ordination rites – to ministry as mere ethical commitment to be humble and morally earnest (Burrows 1980: 69). I see "servant leadership" rhetoric as sometimes engaging in such reductionism. John N. Collins's research further calls such rhetoric into question.

The field of missiology has struggled with *diakonia* in several ways, but perhaps most directly in our definitional concerns about how ministry and mission are interrelated. Is ministry (*diakonia*) a subset of activity done by specifically or generally commissioned persons *on behalf of* the community which, as a whole, participates in the broader *missio Dei*, or is mission a subset of activity – "mission in the dimension of difference" – with ministry being just about everything individuals or the church does? At the risk of being somewhat reductionist myself, I see John N. Collins and Paul Avis representing the "ministry-as-subset-of mission" view and

Titus Presler representing the "mission-as-subset-of ministry" view (Avis 2005; Collins 1990; Presler 2010). My own view probably comes closest to that expressed by Paul Avis. He simultaneously refers to mission as a broad concept and also a concept more limited to "cutting edge" activities. For Avis, "[m]ission is the whole Church bringing the whole Christ to the whole world. In this holistic concept of mission, mission is seen as the cutting edge of the total life of the Church" (Avis 2005: 1).

For missiologists what is at stake here is also related to the decades-long debate (now somewhat muted or taking a different shape in an ethos of anti-institutional attitudes) between the interrelationship of ecclesiology with missiology. In the 1960s this was simplistically expressed in the contrast between "God-church-world" and "God-world-church" framing of how the *Missio Dei* ought best be understood. (The debate between Hoekendijk and McGavran on this does not need to be pointed out for this audience of missiologists.) How one conceptualizes ministry (*diakonia*) as either a subset of mission or as the more encompassing term than mission reflexively influences and is influenced by one's ecclesiology.

For this paper, my intent is not to rehearse the missiological debates around so-called ecclesiocentrism and liberal expressions of the *missio Dei* of the early to mid-20th century (expressed, respectively, at Tambaram in 1938 and Uppsala in 1968) or even to wade into the debate about how mission and ministry might best be defined. Rather, I want to focus on the ambiguity surrounding *diakonia* specifically. This debate is reasonably well known by theologians and church leaders in Europe and northern-European influenced denominations and federations; Lutheran World Federation and Porvoo Agreement denominations know this debate best (Hanover Report of the Anglican-Lutheran International Commission 1996; Dietrich, Jorgensen, Korslien, and Nordstokke 2014). The debate around *diakonia* is almost entirely unknown by American evangelicals, a group well-represented among our APM colleagues. Roman Catholics, United Methodists, and Anglicans have scholars who have addressed the matter extensively, but the extent to which their ideas have influenced others in their churches is difficult to tell (Avis 2005; Collins 1990; 2006; Gooder 2006; Hartley 2004).

To be clear, my contribution in this paper is primarily to call for more conversation in missiological circles about the contested nature of the biblical term for ministry – *diakonia* – as it is being used in a number of academic programs in Europe which for Americans might be seen as programs in mission or "holistic ministry." How we talk about *diakonia* makes a difference in whether and how missiologists build partnerships with denominations and training institutes that use the term *diakonia* as a constitutive dimension of God's mission. Training centers such as the Diakoniewissenschaftliches Institut at the University of Heidelberg is probably the most long-standing and research-focused diaconal institute in Europe, but similar institutes also exist in other European countries (Norway, Czech Republic, Finland). I believe missiology has an especially important gift to offer these regions where the church seeks to be faithful in addressing its "asymmetrical burden" in the midst of European secularity. Understanding *diakonia* is integral to being faithful in that context (Schreiter 2010). Our understanding of *diakonia* also influences the ministry of deacons in our churches, a ministry which Paul Avis describes as "at the same time the most problematic and the most promising of all the ministries of the Church" (Avis 2009: 3).

I look forward to hearing from conference participants about how you are navigating the terrain around the term *diakonia* in the contexts in which you serve. How are you experiencing – if at all – the ambiguity which surround this term in your own academic programs or denominations? Is this a problem primarily for Lutheran and Lutheran-influenced groups? In the school where I work we have just barely begun to grapple with this problem in our "Open Seminary" program which utilizes a number of biblical Greek terms as an interpretive framework for its curriculum. One of those terms is *diakonia*. In my own denomination of the United Methodist Church I seem to be serving in a kind of mediating role between two different understandings of *diakonia* and have been trying to negotiate those differences for almost twenty years. As mostly a historian of mission, the few times I have authored explicitly theological articles in the last fifteen years have mostly been occasions where I focused on this question (Hartley 1999; 2003; 2004; 2014; Hartley and Van Buren 1999).[1]

Conceptually, the ambiguity surrounding the meaning and practice of *diakonia* might be best characterized as an ellipse which – for the geometrically uninitiated – is defined as an elongated circle with two gravitational centers. The various sorts of discourse about *diakonia* could be seen as constituting the various orbital paths one could take in lesser or

---

1   This has been personally important to me as my calling as a permanent deacon in God's church is a calling that resonates as deeply as my missionary vocation. In fact, I view my diaconal calling as a particular expression of my missionary vocation. Interestingly and somewhat self-critically, my reflections on the diaconate have not always reflexively informed my missiological thinking as much as I think they could have or perhaps should have.

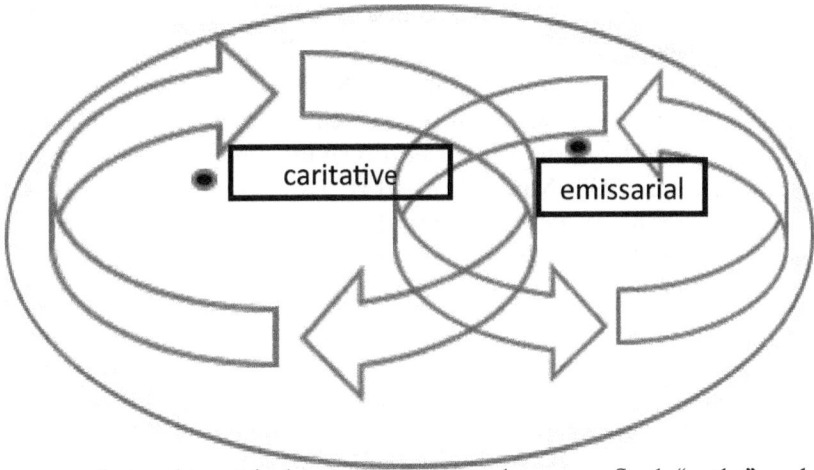

greater relationship with the two gravitational centers. Such "paths" could be depicted with the use of many more arrows than in the figure above. The gravitational centers are the caritative and the emissarial dimensions of meaning for *diakonia*.

Caritative

For most northern European Christians today the term *diakonia* mostly brings to mind the field of meaning which in German is called *diakonie* or religiously-motivated social welfare work – the caritative gravitational center in the figure above. The genesis for this understanding of *diakonia* mostly comes from biblical interpretation of the choosing of the seven in Acts 6 and the tendency of deacons (who were not known as such in Acts 6) by the fourth century to be associated – at least sometimes – with the imagery of the basin and towel (Connolly 1932: 148-150). The understanding of deacons' vocation to be focused on humble, loving service found expression in Luther's and Calvin's ecclesiology as well (Olson 1992: 99-118). In the nineteenth century the association between deacons and social welfare work was strengthened further by the work of Theodor Fliedner and Johann Wichern in their work among the poor which Wichern famously called the church's "Inner Mission."

A one-to-one correspondence developed between deacon's work and loving, humble service such that biblical terms for ministry (*diakonia*, *diakonos*, etc.) similarly took on a strong caritative meaning in German and other European languages. During World War II the diaconal movement in Germany largely acquiesced to the demands of the Nazi party; diaconal workers were, by definition, humble servants after all. Friedrich von Bodelschwingh (1877-1946) was a noteworthy exception to this in his work to save the aged and mentally ill from being classified as "Lebensunwerteslebens" (life unworthy of life) and killed by the Hitler regime (Strohm 1990; Nordstokke 2014). (My own great-grandmother who was severely mentally ill during the war years was so classified and killed.) By the last few decades of the twentieth century a more or less subservient understanding of *diakonia* in northern European languages began to be modified somewhat around the concept of "prophetic diakonia" and an understanding of *diakonia* that sought to infuse a stronger ecclesial dimension into the understanding and practice of *diakonia* (Poser 1987). Juergen Moltmann was one prominent theologian who engaged in theological reflection around the concept of *diakonia* in this period and sought to apply insights from liberation theology to it (Moltmann 1984).

Prominent centers of study around *diakonia* mostly understood in this caritative dimension have been established in a number of European countries. The Diakoniewissenschaftliches Institut at the University of Heidelberg is perhaps one of the most long-standing and influential of these institutes. Some of these institutes have master's level degree programs which acquaint students with the debate surrounding *diakonia* but do not appear to be explicitly missiological in the scholarly resources which they utilize even if their program's description seems to encapsulate much of what the Association of Professors of Mission encourages. The Norwegian Diakonhjemmet University College describes its master's degree in Diakonia and Christian Social Practice as follows:

> After completing the programme you will have…

> Obtained the knowledge of the theory and practice of diakonia, as well as the professional competence required to function within congregations, institutions and organizations. This knowledge includes a basic understanding of Christian theology.

> Acquired an integrated and professional understanding of diaconal approaches and methods that express international and ecumenical awareness, interdisciplinary perspectives, perspectives of participation and gender awareness in relation to diaconal practice.

Gained competency in facing the major contemporary challenges within diaconal action related to the struggle for justice, stewardship of Creation, building inclusive fellowships, and expressing love for one's neighbour.

Developed his/her competence in applying acquired knowledge related to understanding, methods and problem solving – in new and unfamiliar environments (Diakonhjemmet University College, 2015).

In this program description the term "missiological" or "missional" could be readily inserted in place of diaconal. For us in the Association of Professors of Mission it is worth considering why it is not.

Emissarial

The renegotiating of the concept of *diakonia* to be more liberative and prophetic in the 1980s was even more strongly called into question by the landmark linguistic study of *diakonia* and its cognates in the New Testament by John N. Collins's *Diakonia: Reinterpreting the Ancient Sources* (1990). In the twenty-five years since its publication it has prompted considerable re-evaluation of *diakonia* by biblical scholars. To my knowledge, no one has brought forth evidence which seriously counters the claims made by Collins in his 1990 publication. The differences between the older understanding of *diakon-* words and the newer interpretation may be succinctly expressed by comparing the definitions of the term in Bauer's Greek-English Lexicon in the 2nd edition (sometimes denoted by the initials of its authors as BAGD, 1979) with the 3rd edition which directly draws from Collins's work (BDAG, 2001; Gooder 2006: 46-47).

Comparison of Definitions of *diakoneo* in the New Testament in Bauer's Greek-English lexicon[2]	
BAGD 2nd edition (1979)	BDAG 3rd edition (2001)
1) Wait on someone at table	1) To function as an intermediary, act as a go-between/agent, be at one's service with intermediary function either expressed or implied.
2) Serve generally, of services of any kind	2) To perform obligations, without focus on intermediary function.
3) Care for, take care of	3) To meet an immediate need, help.
4) Help, support someone	4) To carry out official duties, minister. Rendering of specific assistance, aid, support (Acts 6:1); send someone something for support (Acts 11:29).
5) Of the ecclesiastical office serve as deacon	5) Acts 6:2 poses a special problem: care for, take care of… "look after tables" can be understood of serving food at tables… but it is improbable that some widows would be deprived of food at a communal meal. The term *diakonia* (verse 1) more probably refers to administrative responsibility, one of whose aspects is concern for widows without specifying the kind of assistance that is allotted.

There are three insights which are critical in this shift of *diakon-* word definitions in the New Testament (c.f. Avis 2005; Hannaford 1996; Collins 1992; 2002). First, there has been a significant change in understanding these terms for ministry such that their field of meaning is increasingly focused on intermediary or emissarial relationships of persons and less on the caring, ethical, nature of the acts performed, such as in taking care of or helping someone.[3] It is the relationship with and to the church that is critical to recover here *not* the officious status which may be associated with terms such as emissary or ambassador. Ministry is something that is given to someone by the church; calling something "my ministry" is thus, strictly speaking, an oxymoron (Avis 2005: 46).[4] Ministry is something which the Church may give to an individual (whether lay or ordained) as a public expression of the Church's mission in the world. Something could be designated a ministry through an informal public approval or through a service of ordination; the point is that the work is in some way accountable to the Church. For missiologists this understanding of ministry carries with it the long history of missionary orders which may be especially useful in infusing strength in what has sometimes become a rather anemic understanding of ministry.

Second, as already suggested, the revised definition of *diakon-* terms introduces a greater focus on the missionary meaning of the term such that *diakonos* (minister) is more closely related to *apostolos* (messenger) than our previous understanding of *diakon-*terms have tended to permit with its focus on lowly, humble, service (Schmittals 1969; Braaten 1985). Paula Gooder has underscored that the *diakon-* terms still maintain a sense of menial service in some New Testament passages. However, even when menial service is emphasized as part of a minister's vocation it is still very much related to the minister's emissarial relationship to an authority – and ultimately to Christ as his missionary (Gooder 2006: 46). At a personal level, a more apostolic understanding of a minister's

---

2   The table above is a much-abbreviated depiction of an extensive comparison in two editions of a Greek-English lexicon which also contains definitions of other *daikon* - cognates such as *diakonia* and *diakonos*. For serious examination of these definitions please consult Bauer (1979) and Bauer and Danker (2001).

3   I have only included the verb *diakoneo* in the table above but similar contrasts are evident in related terms *diakonos* and *diakonia*.

4   A fruitful trajectory of reflection to explore here would be the interrelationship between vocation and ministry – for pastors and others (c.f. Hunter 2003; Placher 2005).

vocation may further guard against an unhealthy victim complex whereby one perceives oneself as a burned-out servant of the people more than a sent emissary of God. I believe that the old understanding of *diakonia* and the attendant "servant leader" language is especially vulnerable to such a distortion of ministry – especially if it is left ambiguous whose servant one is (Dulles 1987; McCrimmon 2014). Instead, what is emphasized in the revised understanding of *diakonia* – and, of course, elsewhere in the New Testament – is that one can be radically free to perform menial and self-sacrificial missionary service precisely because of the "high calling" and close emissarial relationship and friendship one can have as a *diakonos* or minister of Jesus.

In a similar way, the older definition of *diakonia* has contributed to wider problematic ecclesial self-understandings. The missionary impulse of the reign of God does not consist in a timid humility of a "let the world set the agenda" variety as the World Council of Churches proclaimed in 1968. In this appeal the WCC was motivated in part by a well-intentioned desire to correct the abuses of ecclesiastical hubris. The diaconate was seen as a vehicle to accomplish this in the Church (Morche 1996). Indeed, ecclesiastical hubris must be rejected, but in doing so one must not be dismissive of the Church (Hannaford 2000: 239-279). An embrace of a revised definition for *diakon-* terms, while of course not refuting true Christian humility, may help the diaconate (and the Church as a whole) embrace the radical missionary values of God's reign whereby the whole Church brings the whole Christ to the whole world.[5] Deacons, deaconess-<u>es, and missioner</u>s cross boundaries with and for the Gospel;[6] they do not

5   Of course, in a very important sense it is not the Church that brings Christ to places and people where he is totally absent. Nor is it the case that the Church is equated with God's reign. The Church participates in God's mission through Christ and in the power of the Holy Spirit. And yet Christians affirm that the Church is also far from being merely incidental in accomplishing God's mission in the world.

6   I am very conscious of the fact that such language of "boundary crossing" is received by some persons as linguistic remnants of a colonial enterprise. I believe that much theological discourse about boundaries and mission needs to be reframed in light of insights gained from postcolonial theory and other sources. I have found David Bosch's essay on the "vulnerability of mission" to be especially useful in my teaching in this regard. Bosch notes that "the activities of adherents of any religion which holds that it has a message of universal validity will invoke images of paternalism. And since the Christian faith, as I have suggested, is intrinsically missionary, it will often be experienced as paternalistic even where it is not. This is, if you wish, simply an "occupational hazard" of

follow an ambiguous or secular "world" which calls the shots for its lowly servants.[7]

A third insight which may be garnered from this new definition of *diakon-* terms is best framed in a negative way: Ministry is not synonymous with activities of Christian discipleship. There has been a rather widespread ecumenical tendency since the 1950s to expand the meaning of ministry to the service of all baptized believers (Poser 1986; Collins 2006). This resulted in nearly everything being identified as a ministry with little left to be considered a matter of Christian discipleship. Loving one's neighbor, caring for the poor, and proclaiming the Gospel of Jesus Christ are activities all Christians ought to do as a matter of their discipleship and are not necessarily ministries – *although they could be*. As Paul Avis argues, all baptized Christians are *potential* ministers even if not all Christians are, by virtue of their baptism, ministers (Avis 2005: 52). As ecclesially accountable leaders missionaries and others are called to encourage and support the serious discipleship of others whether their activities are recognized by the Church (and therefore ministry) or not.

I believe the new interpretive direction opened up by John N. Collins is rich with missiological opportunity. This is perhaps most strikingly expressed in Collins's paraphrased interpretation of the choosing of the seven in Acts 6.

> The Greek-speaking members of the community complained against those who spoke Aramaic that their housebound widows were being overlooked in the great preaching (*diakonia*) that was going on day by day in the environs of the Temple. So the Twelve summoned the whole complement of the disciples and said: 'We cannot possibly break off our public proclamation before the huge crowds in the Temple to carry out a ministry (*diakonein*) in the households of these Greek-speaking widows. Brothers, you will have to choose seven men from your own ethnic group who are fully respected, empowered by the Spirit, and equipped for the task. We will then appoint

Christian missionaries (Bosch 1994: 83)." Bill Burrows is helpful in this regard as well (2010). Among United Methodists, Hendrik Pieterse provides a helpful discussion of the way the UMC uses theological language as a worldwide church (2013).

7   Paul's description of himself and others as slaves (*doulos*) of Christ highlights an honorific element alongside the menial in a similar way to the revised definition of *diakon-* terms (c. f. Martin 1990).

them to the role that needs to be filled. That will mean that the Twelve can get on with attending to worship in the Temple and to our apostolic ministry (*diakonia*) of proclaiming the Word there (Collins 2002: 58).

Even though I think Collins's interpretation of Act 6 and other passages hold a great deal of promise, it is also true that *diakonia* understood in this new way is vulnerable to being misunderstood. Collins's interpretation of *diakonia* in no way calls for retrenchment to "take back" ministry from laypersons and give it exclusively to those who have been ordained. Accountability – a key dimension of a go-between's or emissary's calling – can take many different forms and can be informal or formal in nature.

Conclusion

Our current intellectual context with regard to the understanding and practice of *diakonia* – understood both as religiously motivated social work and as a Greek term in the New Testament for ministry – does not seem to be moving very quickly toward resolving the ambiguity of this word's usage. We seem to be at different places on our ellipse trying to make sense of one another's orbital paths as best we can. Whether this ambiguity will soon be resolved is impossible to predict. Until then, it is important for missiologists and especially professors of mission to at least be aware that there is ambiguity here so that institutional partnerships, ecumenical relationships, and even personal relationships might be initiated or strengthened and not side-tracked by misunderstanding. It would be a tragically ironic thing indeed for ministry to be stymied because of confusion over *diakonia*.

References Cited

Avis, Paul.
    2005   *A Ministry Shaped by Mission*. London: T & T Clark.

    2009   "Editorial: Wrestling witih the Diaconate," *Ecclesiology* 5,
            3-6.

Bauer, Walter
    1979   *A Greek-English lexicon of the New Testament and other
            Early Christian Literature*. Chicago: University of
            Chicago Press.

Bauer, Walter and Frederick William Danker, eds.
    2001   *A Greek-English Lexicon of the New Testament and other
            Early Christian Literature*, Third ed. Chicago: University
            of Chicago Press.

Bosch, David J.
    1992   "The Vulnerability of Mission," in James A. Scherer and
            Stephen B. Bevans, eds. *New Directions in Mission and
            Evangelization 2: Theological Foundations*. Maryknoll, NY:
            Orbis, 73-86.

Braaten, Carl E.
    1985   *The Apostolic Imperative: Nature and Aim of the Church's
            Mission and Ministry*. Minneapolis: Augsburg Fortress
            Publishers.

Burrows, William R.
    1980   *New Ministries: The Global Context*. Maryknoll, NY:
            Orbis Books.

2010   "Moving Beyond Christian Imperialism to Mission as
        Reconciliation with all Creation," in Amos Yong and
        Barbara Brown Zikmund, eds. *Remembering Jamestown:
        Hard Questions about Christian Mission.* Eugene, OR:
        Wipf & Stock, 145-156.

Collins, John N.
    1990   *Diakonia: Reinterpreting the Ancient Sources.* New York:
            Oxford University Press.

    1992   *Are All Christians Ministers?* Collegeville, MN: The
            Liturgical Press.

    2002   *Deacons and the Church: Making Connections between Old
            and New.* Harrisburg, PA: Morehouse Publishing.

    2006   "Ordained and Other Ministries: Making a Difference,"
            Ecclesiology 3 no. 1, 11-32.

Connolly, Hugh
    1932   *Didascalia Apostolorum: The Syriac Version Translated
            and accompanied by the Verona Latin Fragments.* Oxford:
            Clarendon Press.

Diakonhjemmet University College
    2015.   Program description: http://www.diakonhjemmet.no/
            DUC/Studiehaandbok/Direkte-publisering/Studiekat-
            alog/Informasjon/Master-s-Degree-in-Diakonia-and-
            Christian-Social-Practice. Accessed 12 May 2015.

Dietrich, Stephanie, Jorgensen, Knud, Korslien, Kari Karsrud, and
Nordstokke, Kjell, eds.
    2014   *Diakonia as Christian Social Practice: An Introduction.*
            Eugene, OR: Wipf & Stock.

Dulles, Avery
    1987   *Models of the Church,* Expanded ed. New York:
            Doubleday.

Gooder, Paula
    2006   "Diakonia in the New Testament: A Dialogue with John
            N. Collins," *Ecclesiology* 3 no. 1, 33-56.

Hannaford, Robert
  1996   "Foundations for an Ecclesiology of Ministry," in
          Christine Hall and Robert Hannaford, eds. in *Order and
          Ministry*. Leominster, UK: Gracewing.

  2000   "The Representative and Relational Nature of Ministry
          and the Renewal of the Diaconate" in Gunnel
          Borgegard, Olav Fanuelsen, and Christine Hall, eds.
          The Ministry of the Deacon 2: Ecclesiological Explorations.
          Uppsala, Sweden: Nordic Ecumenical Council, 239-279.

Hartley, Benjamin L.
  1999   "Deacons as Emissary-Servants: A Liturgical Theology."
          Quarterly Review, 19 no. 4, 372-386.

  2003   *An Empirical Look at the Ecumenical Diaconate in
          the United States.* (Vol. Monograph Series No. 16).
          Providence, RI: North American Association for the
          Diaconate.

  2004   "Connected and Sent Out: Implications of New
          Biblical Research for the United Methodist Diaconate."
          Quarterly Review, 24 no. 4, 367-380.

  2014   "What's in a Word?" Diakonia and Deacons in the Bible
          and Today," Paper presentation at the United Methodist
          Office of Deaconess and Home Missioner Conference
          on Lay Order, Nashville, TN 26-28 September.

Hartley, Ben L. and Paul Van Buren
  1999   *The Deacon: Ministry through Words of Faith and Acts of
          Love.* Nashville: General Board of Higher Education and
          Ministry, The United Methodist Church.

Hunter, Victor
  2003   *Desert Hearts and Healing Fountains: Gaining Pastoral
          Vocational Clarity.* St. Louis: Chalice Press.

Hanover Report of the Anglican-Lutheran International Commission
  1996   *The Diaconate as Ecumenical Opportunity.* Anglican Con-
          sultative Council and the Lutheran World Federation.

Lutheran World Federation
    2009   *Diakonia in Context: Transformation, Reconciliation, Empowerment. An LWF Contribution to the Understanding and Practice of Diakonia.* Geneva: LWF, 2009.

Martin, Dale
    1990   *Slavery as Salvation: The Metaphor of Slavery in Pauline Christianity* New Haven: Yale University Press.

McCrimmon, Mitch
    2014   "Why Servant Leadership is a Bad Idea," http://www.management-issues.com/opinion/6015/why-servant-leadership-is-a-bad-idea/. Accessed 19 July 2014.

Moltmann, Juergen
    1984   *Diakonie im Horizont des Reiches Gottes.* Neukirchen-Vluyn: Neukirchener Verlag.

Morche, Margret
    1996   *Zur Erneuerung des Staendigen Diakonats: Ein Beitrag zur Geschichte unter besonderer Beruecksichtigung der Arbeit des Internationalen Diakonatszentrums in seiner Verbindung zum Deutschen Caritasverband.* Freiburg im Breisgau: Lambertus Verlag.

Nordstokke, Kjell
    2014   "The Study of Diakonia as an Academic Discipline," In Stephanie Dietrich, Knud Jorgensen, Kari Karsrud Korslien and Kjell Nordstokke, eds., *Diakonia as Christian Social Practice: An Introduction.* Eugene, OR: Wipf & Stock.

Olson, Jeannine E.
    1992   *One Ministry Many Roles: Deacons and Deaconesses through the Centuries.* St. Louis, MO: Concordia.

Pieterse, Hendrik R.
    2013   "A Worldwide United Methodist Church? Soundings toward a Connectional Theological Imagination" *Methodist Review* 5.

Placher, William C.
2005   *Callings: Twenty Centuries of Christian Wisdom on Vocation.* Grand Rapids: Eerdmans.

Poser, Klaus (Ed.)
1987   *Diakonia 2000: Called to be Neighbours, Official Report, WCC World Consultation Inter-Church Aid, Refugee and World Service, Larnaca, 1986.* Geneva: WCC Publications.

Presler, Titus
2010   "Mission is Ministry in the Dimension of Difference: A Definition for the Twenty-first Century." *International Bulletin of Missionary Research, 34*(4), 195-204.

Schmithals, Walter
1969   *The Office of Apostle in the Early Church.* Nashville: Abingdon Press.

Schreiter, Robert
2010   "Mission from the Ground Up: Emergent Themes in Contemporary Mission," in Ogbu U. Kalu, Peter Vethanayagamony, and Edmund Kee-Fook Chia eds. *Mission after Christendom: Emergent Themes in Contemporary Mission.* Louisville, KY: Westminster John Knox Press, 12-24.

Strohm, Theodor
1990   *Diakonie im 'Dritten Reich'.* Heidelberg: Heidelberger Verlaganstalt.

Mission Studies as Evangelization and Theology for World Christianity

Reflections on Mission Studies in Britian and Ireland, 2000 - 2015

KIRSTEEN KIM

DOI: 10.7252/Paper. 000051

About the Author

Kirsteen Kim, Ph.D., is Professor of Theology and World Christianity at Leeds Trinity University. Kirsteen researches and teaches theology from the perspective of mission and world Christianity, drawing on her experience of Christianity while living and working in South Korea, India and the USA, with a special interest in theology of the Holy Spirit. She publishes widely and is the editor of *Mission Studies*, the journal of the International Association for Mission Studies.

Foreword

In 2000 and in 2012 I published papers for the British and Irish Association for Mission Studies (BIAMS) on mission studies in Britain and Ireland, which were published in journals of theological education.[1] These two papers surveyed the state of mission studies and how in this region it is related to various other disciplines. Each paper suggested a next stage in the development of mission studies: the first saw mission studies as facilitating a worldwide web of missiological discussion; the second suggested that mission studies should be appreciated as internationalizing theology more generally. This article reviews the developments in Britain and Ireland over the years which are detailed in these articles and bring them up to date. It further argues that, while continuing to develop as "mission studies" or "missiology", the discipline should today claim the names "theology for world Christianity" and "studies in evangelization."

Introduction to a World-Wide Web (2000)

British and Irish Association for Mission Studies

In the 1984 Conference of ACATE, the Association of Adult Centres of Theological Education, that "every curriculum ought to find some place for the study of the theology of mission."[2] In response to this call, The British and Irish Association for Mission Studies (BIAMS) was founded in 1989 to promote the study of mission as a recognized discipline within

1   Kirsteen Kim "Mission Studies in Britain and Ireland: Introduction to a World-wide Web", *British Journal of Theological Education*, 11.1 (2000), 72-86; "Mission Studies in Britain and Ireland: Internationalising Theology," *Journal of Adult Theological Education* 8.2 (2012), 130-52.

2   See Kenneth Cracknell and Christopher Lamb, *Theology on Full Alert* (London: British Council of Churches, rev. ed, 1986), pp. 1-2, 132-35.

theological education at the instigation of a consortium of Anglican mission agencies—Partnership for World Mission—and the General Synod Board for Mission and Unity of the Church of England.[3] In the succeeding decade BIAMS made further links with universities, colleges and training institutions and strengthened its church connections through a close relationship with the Churches' Commission on Mission, an ecumenical body. BIAMS drew together both practitioners and theorists of mission[4] at biennial conferences interspersed with day conferences.[5] It stimulated interest in mission studies by a twice-yearly *Newsletter*, website, and interest groups.

Mission studies as a theological and academic discipline

In a paper written with the help of the then BIAMS executive and published in 2000, I argued that mission studies was an established theological and academic discipline in the UK. It was represented in some shape or form in most theological colleges and in many university departments in Britain and Ireland. The main university centers were Birmingham, Edinburgh, and Cambridge. The University of Birmingham Department of Theology claimed to be the first in the country to focus on the study of mission and world Christianity and had the only chair of mission in Britain or Ireland.[6] New College, University of Edinburgh claimed a double distinction in the history of mission studies. It was the venue for the great World Missionary Conference of 1910 and had what has been called "the first chair of mission studies anywhere in the Protestant world."[7] The Centre for the Study of Christianity in the Non-Western

---

3   Timothy Yates, "Edinburgh 1990—'New Prospects for Mission': An Inaugural Event in Mission Studies", *Anvil 8/2* (1991), pp. 123-29.

4   Timothy Yates, Editorial, *BIAMS Newsletter* 13 (Sept. 1999), 3.

5   BIAMS was constituted at Edinburgh in 1990, which reflected on mission studies in the light of Edinburgh 1910, eighty years before.

6   It was held jointly by the Department and the School of Mission at the Selly Oak Colleges. In 2000 the chair was occupied by Werner Ustorf and previously by Walter Hollenweger.

7   This was occupied by Alexander Duff (its architect) in 1867 but disappeared before the end of the century. Andrew Walls, "Missiological Education in Historical Perspective", J. Dudley Woodberry, Charles Van Engen and Edgar J. Elliston (eds.), *Missiological Education for the 21st Century: The Book, the*

World founded by Andrew Walls was based in the Faculty of Divinity.[8] The Henry Martyn Centre,[9] an associate institute of the Cambridge Theological Federation, was a foundational resource for research projects in the Faculty[10] and for courses on mission and world Christianity taught in the University and Federation. There were substantial archives of mission societies in the UK concentrated principally at the Universities of London (SOAS), Leeds, Birmingham, Cambridge, Edinburgh and Oxford.[11] Two academic journals of mission were being published: *Studies in World Christianity* at the University of Edinburgh and *Transformation*, "an international evangelical dialogue on mission and ethics" based at the Oxford Centre for Mission Studies. There were specialist publishers for mission studies: SPCK in the UK and Columba Press in Ireland.

Mission studies and other disciplines

No one had done more to establish mission studies as a theological and academic discipline than the South African missiologist David Bosch.[12] Nearly a decade after its publication, Bosch's *Transforming Mission* looked set to remain the indispensable *summa missiologica* and Bosch's broad view of mission, "biblical, and systematic, and historical, and practical"[13] was

---

Circles and the Sandals (Maryknoll, NY: Orbis, 1996), 11-17. Duff's chair was actually entitled "evangelistic theology" but Walls argues that the scope which Duff proposed for it corresponds to "missiology" today, pp. 12-13.

8   The director at that time was David Kerr.

9   Founding director Graham Kings.

10 The North Atlantic Missiology Project and Currents in World Christianity (1996-2001), both directed by Brian Stanley.

11 An indication of this is that in 1999 these universities received a joint grant of £415,000 from the Research Support Libraries Programme to accelerate, extend and improve access to their missionary collections.

12 On whose work the BIAMS conference at Lampeter in 1993 focused.

13 Andrew Walls, "Missiologist of the Road: David Jacobus Bosch (1929-1992)", *BIAMS Newsletter* 2 (March 1994), pp. 1-5.

largely accepted. Nevertheless uncertainty about the nature of mission lingered,[14] together with questions about what constitutes mission studies and where it should it fit in the theological curriculum.

Since the study of mission depended on interfaces with a wide range of disciplines, the paper surveyed the main partners of mission studies in the UK and Ireland to illustrate its scope, serve as an introduction to the subject, and show its importance to the theological curriculum. These were:

a) The interface with behavioral sciences and with communications when treated as evangelism, with the emphasis on the proclamation and translation of the message.

b) The use of social studies when missiology is a partner of development studies and it relates to social justice, peace studies and ecology, the prophetic voice of mission.[15]

c) The historical study of missionary activity, which is a particular strength in the UK because of the presence of so many archives. Although of growing interest to secular historians, Timothy Yates argued it is best done by holding theology and history in tension.[16]

d) The interface with religious studies and theology of religions. This was providing much of the impetus for study of mission in Britain because of rising awareness of the presence of significant numbers of people of other faiths.[17]

---

14 As suggested by the title of J. Andrew Kirk, *What is Mission? Theological Explorations* (London: Darton, Longman and Todd, 1999).

15 The 1995 BIAMS conference "Mission on Trial" at Bearsden, Glasgow, asked whether the church was guilty of collusion in an unjust global economy and discussed how *kerygma, koinonia,* and *diakonia* can be held in creative inter-relationship in mission. Timothy Yates, Editorial, *BIAMS Newsletter* 6 (March 1996), 1-3.

16 Timothy Yates, *Christian Mission in the Twentieth Century* (Cambridge: CUP, 1994), 3-6.

17 This is clear from the case studies in Cracknell and Lamb, *Theology on Full Alert.*

e) The study of mission through cultural anthropology and cultural studies[18] was seen as foundational to mission studies as missionaries have adapted themselves to other cultures and attempted to express the gospel in indigenous terms.[19] Furthermore, the challenge of Lesslie Newbigin in the 1980s to "a genuinely missionary encounter" with modernity had raised the awareness of "our culture."[20]

f) The close relationship of missiology and ecumenics, with which at that time in Europe it was often twinned. This reflected the fact that the ecumenical movement grew out of the missionary movement and the insight of the *missio Dei* paradigm that mission results in ingathering.[21]

g) The bringing together of mission and biblical studies, which had opened the way to studies of the biblical foundations for mission that did not depend merely on the Great Commission passages but on the thrust of Scripture as a whole.[22] Mission studies was also conscious of the

---

18   The ambiguous relation of mission and cultures was recognized in the BIAMS conference at All Nations Christian College, Ware, in 1991 which looked at "Christ, Culture, and Columbus" and highlighted the necessity for a positive appreciation of cultural difference and the validity of other ways of life if mission is to be practiced in a Christ-like manner.

19   For a comprehensive study of inculturation by a British missiologist, see Aylward Shorter, *Towards a Theology of Inculturation* (London: Chapman, 1988).

20   See e.g., Lesslie Newbigin, *The Gospel in a Pluralist Society* (London: SPCK, 1989). An obituary to Newbigin written by his biographer Eleanor Jackson can be found in *BIAMS Newsletter* 10 (March 1998), 1-2.

21   See David Bosch, *Transforming Mission: Paradigm Shifts in Theology of Mission* (Maryknoll, NY: Orbis Books, 1991), 368-393.

22   The importance of the missionary motif in biblical studies is recognized in the work of such contemporary British biblical scholars as Richard Bauckham, Christopher Rowland, and Christopher J.H. Wright.

re-reading of the Bible from non-Western contexts as developed in post-colonial interpretations or intercultural hermeneutics.[23]

Mission studies interfaced with systematic or dogmatic theology in both theology of mission and the development of a missionary theology.[24] The study of Third World theologies[25] or Non-Western theologies[26] emerged naturally out of study of mission. It not only contained a critique of Western models of mission[27] but suggested that the issues for theology in the new millennium would be pioneered outside the West.

Mission studies and theological education

I argued that, as a recognized discipline, mission studies should be a subject in the theological curriculum in its own right; it would be impoverished if reduced to one of its constituent parts or squeezed into a narrow section of the theological curriculum. Furthermore, "the dimensional aspect" of missiology, that is its task of highlighting theology's reference to the world, means that a missionary perspective should also permeate all theological disciplines.[28] And the questions raised by mission

---

23   See, e.g. R.S. Sugirtharajah, *Asian Biblical Hermeneutics and Post-Colonialism: Contrasting the Interpretations* (Sheffield: Sheffield Academic Press: 1999).

24   Bosch, *Transforming Mission*, 492-96. The 1999 BIAMS conference at St Stephen's College, Oxford, invited Jürgen Moltmann, a theologian with a missionary perspective, to what proved to be a very lively debate with Theo Sundermeier, a missiologist, on the theme "Mission—an Invitation to God's Future".

25   John Parratt, University of Birmingham.

26   Andrew Walls, University of Edinburgh.

27   Mention has already been made of Edinburgh's CSCNWW and the recognition of the subject at the University of Birmingham. The University of Cambridge also had a Christianity in Asia Project (1997-2001). See Sebastian Kim (ed.), *Christian Theology in Asia* (Cambridge: CUP, 2008).

28   Cf. Bosch, *Transforming Mission*, 489-98.

studies about the contextual nature of theology mean that missiology is party to the post-modern critique of theology, as Bosch demonstrated.[29] In this sense missiology appeared to represent the future of theology. At the High Leigh conference (1984), Kenneth Cracknell and Christopher Lamb drew attention to what they saw as parochialism in British theology, "its enclosure within an exclusively European, not to say Anglo-Saxon, cultural framework" and the "timeless and uncontextualized" nature of much theology teaching.[30] They had suggested that mission studies, by the boundary-breaking nature of mission itself, is an important factor in overcoming these limitations. In the newly electronically globalized era, I suggested that the study of mission is an introduction to a world-wide web. It is a subject which crosses theological and academic boundaries in its reflection on the mission of God to the world expressed in the living Word and the life-giving Spirit.

I concluded the article with the words of Orlando Costas, who highlighted the way in which missiology challenges mainstream theology:

> Missiology contends against all theological provincialism, advocating an intercultural perspective in theology. Missiology questions all theological discourse that does not seriously consider the missionary streams of the Christian faith; all biblical interpretation that ignores the missionary motives that shape biblical faith; all history of Christianity that omits the expansion of Christianity across cultural, social, and religious frontiers; and all pastoral theology that does not take seriously the mandate to communicate the Gospel fully and to the heart of the concrete situations of daily life.... By fulfilling such a

---

29   Although whether Bosch's paradigm was post - modern is questionable—see Kirsteen Kim, "Post-Modern Mission: A Paradigm Shift in David Bosch's Theology of Mission?" *International Review of Mission* 89/353 (2000), 172–179.

30   Cracknell and Lamb, *Theology on Full Alert*, 8, 15.

critical task, missiology also enriches theology because it puts theology in contact with the worldwide Church with all its cultural and theological diversity.[31]

Internationalizing Theology (2012)

In the twelve years between the first and second survey, the world had changed significantly. The first article was published before the events of 9/11 (2001), and the British equivalent 7/7 (2005), before the credit crunch and the Euro crisis, before the election of Barack Obama or David Cameron, and before China became the world's second largest economy. Since mission is inextricably related to context, I argued, the changing global landscape must lead to changes in mission studies. Another important factor driving change in mission studies was the state of higher education in Britain and Ireland and the diminishing place of Christian theology within it. The second article aimed to update the earlier one and sketch the current state of mission studies in these nations in light of these developments as well as others which are more internal to the churches in these nations. The article looked at the changing nature of mission studies, the changing location of mission in the academy, and the changing content of mission studies.[32] And, picking up from the conclusion of the earlier paper, it ended by asking whether and to what the extent mission studies and its changing nature impacted the teaching and study of theology in Britain and Ireland.

---

31   Orlando E. Costas, "Theological Education and Mission" in C. René Padilla (ed.), *New Alternatives in Theological Education* (Oxford: Regnum Books, 1988), 5-24 (p. 15).

32   The author acknowledged the advice of Wonsuk Ma, Nigel Rooms and Cathy Ross in finalising this article.

Challenges and opportunities for mission studies

Decline of the study of mission as a focused subject

Since the year 2000, the place of mission studies in universities, colleges and research institutions had changed and relations between bodies had been reconfigured. University departments of theology continued the trend toward diversifying into "theology and religious studies". Where there had been integration between the two disciplines, the Christian input developed into Christian studies and theology was no longer only Christian theology. Amid continued political anxiety to identify common ground among the religions, the missionary dimensions of faiths tended to be neglected. Mission studies seemed to have lost its (admittedly tenuous) foothold as a distinct discipline. The Centre for Mission Studies at the University of Birmingham, a legacy of the Selly Oak Colleges had closed and the chair in mission was not occupied. Two Catholic centers for mission studies had closed: the Missionary Institute London, which was affiliated to the Universities of Middlesex and Leuven, and Kimmage Mission Institute, Dublin. The University of Leeds, which during the time of Adrian Hastings produced many doctorates in mission and world Christianity, no longer reflected that orientation. However, there were still bright spots. The Oxford Centre for Mission Studies had been revived by Wonsuk Ma and continued to attract students for postgraduate degrees, but most were from overseas and this power house of global mission thinking was not really engaged with the British churches. The Irish School of Ecumenics at Trinity College, Dublin specialized in the world mission-related topics of intercultural theology and interreligious studies, international peace studies, and conflict resolution and reconciliation. The number of masters programs in mission validated by universities had actually increased.[33] Much of this was driven by the growth of church-planting initiatives. This suggested that in the colleges training for Christian ministry mission studies was increasingly mainstream.[34]

Shift from world mission to local mission

The most noteworthy change in the nature of mission studies was that in the space of less than twenty years the meaning of the word "mission" in the British churches had gone from being used almost exclusively for overseas work to referring primarily to the outreach work of local churches in Britain. The British and Irish Association for Mission Studies (BIAMS) was founded in 1989 to study the history, theology and practice of mission and to encourage awareness of the major issues in contemporary mission. BIAMS was to serve a consortium of churches and mission agencies, which were known for their activities overseas, so when its constitution was approved the following year no one thought to specify that the study of mission should have a global dimension – that was a given. Yet only fifteen years later, under the influence particularly of the Gospel in Our Culture Network and the missional church movement, the use of the word "mission" in Britain had become so focused on the local context that a global interest could no longer be taken for granted. Moreover, the long-term decline in missionary sending and the problems of the partnership model had led to the demise of the umbrella bodies that had founded BIAMS. In order to try to hold together local mission in Britain and the

---

33   These included Redcliffe College, Gloucester; Cliff College, Derbyshire; Springdale College, Selly Oak; All Nations Christian College, Ware; the Queen's Foundation, Birmingham; Trinity College Bristol.

34   The author verified this in the case of the six colleges affiliated to Queen's University Belfast, the Queen's Foundation in Birmingham, the Yorkshire Ministry Course based at Mirfield, St Michael's Llandaff, and Ripon College Cuddesdon. Further evidence is the publication by the main specialist theology publisher, SCM, of Stephen Spencer, *Christian Mission: SCM Study Guide* (London: SCM Press, 2007).

wider world church, at its conference in 2005, BIAMS found it necessary to amend its Constitution by including "worldwide" in the description of mission.

Mission and world Christianity

Although mission studies had declined in the universities, "world Christianity" was proving acceptable because it did not have the same colonial baggage as "mission." Mission studies that takes its global context seriously is clearly linked to the study of world Christianity. However, there is a danger that the study of world Christianity is presented as the successor to mission studies because it is seen as the fruit of colonial missions which had planted churches in every continent. I argued that mission, and its study, continues to be highly relevant even in the era of world Christianity for two main reasons. First, because world Christianity is not just the result of recent missionary expansion but is a phenomenon that goes back into the New Testament which brings together documents – such as the four Gospels –from a wide geographical area. Second because mission itself has never been entirely a Northern or colonial phenomenon. Every church has its own missionary activity, and world mission is now well established from populous Christian nations in the global South and East, such as Nigeria, Brazil, and Korea.

The prominence of "world Christianity" in Britain and Ireland and elsewhere was largely due to the work of Andrew Walls at Aberdeen, Edinburgh, Princeton, and Liverpool Hope University.[35] There was other significant discussion of the nature and significance of "world Christianity"

---

35   Andrew F. Walls, *The Missionary Movement in Christian History: Studies in the Transmission of Faith* (Maryknoll, NY: Orbis Books, 1996); Andrew F. Walls, *The Cross-cultural Process in Christian History: Studies in the Transmission and Appropriation of Faith* (Maryknoll, NY: Orbis Books, 2002). See also Timothy Yates, *The Expansion of Christianity* (Oxford: Lion Publishing, 2004). For BIAMS discussion on the future of world Christianity, see Timothy Yates (ed.), *Mission and the Next Christendom* (Sheffield: Cliff College, 2005), the papers of the 2005 BIAMS conference.

emanating from the UK context in this period.[36] In 2008, Liverpool Hope University launched a new Andrew F. Walls Centre for the Study of Asian and African Christianity directed by Daniel Jeyaraj, Professor of World Christianity, with significant archives. The former Centre for the Study of Christianity in the Non-Western World at the University of Edinburgh had reduced somewhat in size but continued to attract postgraduate students as the Centre for the Study of World Christianity, led by Brian Stanley. The Henry Martyn Centre in Cambridge under Emma Wild-Wood, and soon to be renamed the Cambridge Centre for Christianity Worldwide, continued to contribute to the teaching of mission to the Cambridge Theological Federation and to develop its important library of books and journals related to mission and world Christianity. Two leading scholars of the sociology of religion in England were treating Christianity in global perspective: Grace Davie at the University of Exeter and Linda Woodhead at the University of Lancaster.

Edinburgh 1910 centenary project

Probably the most significant event in mission studies in the intervening decade was the centenary of the World Missionary Conference of Edinburgh 1910. The research done for the conference a century ago was one of the earliest examples of mission studies and one of the main reasons why Edinburgh 1910 is remembered a century later. Encouraged by the World Council of Churches, for which the Edinburgh conference was a historical milestone, the anniversary project was constructed to highlight

---

36   Sebastian Kim and Kirsteen Kim, *Christianity as a World Religion* (London: Continuum, 2008); Noel Davies and Martin Conway, *World Christianity in the 21ˢᵗ Century* 2 vols. (London: SCM-Canterbury Press 2008).

important mission-related developments over that period: the growth of the ecumenical movement,[37] the rise of awareness of world Christianity,[38] and the consensus around the *missio Dei* paradigm.[39]

The commemoration of Edinburgh 1910 by the Edinburgh 2010 project and conference at the University of Edinburgh was a great but largely unrealized opportunity for mission studies in Britain and Ireland. Brian Stanley, Professor of World Christianity at the University of Edinburgh, produced the definitive history of the 1910 conference[40] and the preparatory volumes and conference report were published by Regnum Books International as part of the Regnum Edinburgh Centenary Series.[41] Although Edinburgh 2010 was a truly global project involving Christians from every region of the world and leaders of global church and mission bodies, British-based missiologists and institutions were very well

---

37   In contrast to 1910, Edinburgh 2010 was not a gathering of Protestants only; its governing body included all the main streams of world Christianity— Catholic, Evangelical, Orthodox, Pentecostal, and Protestant, demonstrating the great strides in ecumenical cooperation in mission. See the Common Call, available at www.edinburgh2010.org.

38   The composition of the research network and conference delegations was intended to include 60 per cent from the global South to represent the proportions identified in Todd Johnson and Kenneth Ross (eds.), *The Atlas of Global Christianity* (Edinburgh: Edinburgh University Press, 2009).

39   This stood for the post-war and post-colonial insight that mission does not belong to the churches but is God's initiative in which we are called to participate in humility and hope. Bosch, *Transforming Mission*, republished in 2011, was taken as still the best exposition of this.

40   Brian Stanley, *The World Missionary Conference, Edinburgh 1910* (Grand Rapids, MI: Wm B. Eerdmans /Cambridge: CUP, 2009).

41   David A. Kerr and Kenneth R. Ross, *Edinburgh 2010: Mission Then and Now* (Oxford: Regnum Books, 2009); Daryl Balia and Kirsteen Kim (eds.), *Edinburgh 2010: Witnessing to Christ Today*, Vol. 2 (Oxford: Regnum Books, 2010); Kirsteen Kim and Andrew Anderson, *Edinburgh 2010: Mission Today and Tomorrow* (Oxford: Regnum Books, 2011). The Regnum Edinburgh Centenary Series has now extended to nearly thirty volumes. See http://www. ocms.ac.uk/regnum/edinburgh. Note also, Ian M. Ellis, *A Century of Mission and Unity: A Centenary Perspective on the Edinburgh 1910 World Missionary Conference* (Blackrock: Columba Press, 2010).

represented in the research project.[42] However, the benefits of hosting the project were not as great as they could have been because of the weakened infrastructure for mission studies and also the tensions between the nations within the United Kingdom.

Changing content of mission studies

In 2012, I found that mission studies was not so much a focus for inter-disciplinary work but rather was carried on under various other headings, particularly ecclesiology, culture, spirituality, interfaith relations, development studies, public affairs, eco-theology and the study of migration.

Mission-shaped church

Undoubtedly the widest and most intense discussion around mission in the first decade of the new century was generated by *Mission-shaped Church*, the report of the Mission and Public Affairs Council of the Church of England in 2004, which called for "a new inculturation of the gospel within our society."[43] Reflection on national social trends led the writers of *Mission-shaped Church* to endorse work already being done in planting churches among networks rather than necessarily in geographically defined locations. And their observation that consumerism is a metaphor for much of contemporary Western culture[44] led them to argue that to reach out in consumer society the church must reshape itself around worshippers as consumers. These were the main reasons for encouraging "fresh expressions of church," a movement which had now diversified

42 British-based missiologists were very well represented in the research project in its inception (Ken Ross), on its steering group (Rose Dowsett, John Kafwanka, Wonsuk Ma), as research coordinator (Kirsteen Kim), and as co-conveners of six out of the nine study themes (Janice Price, Andrew Kirk, Mark Oxbrow, Afe Adogame, Darrell Jackson, Wonsuk Ma and Cathy Ross).

43 Graham Cray (ed.), *Mission-shaped Church: Church Planting and Fresh Expressions of Church in a Changing Context* (London: Church House Publishing, 2004), xii.

44 Building partly on Pete Ward, *Liquid Church* (Carlisle: Paternoster Press, 2002).

to cover all sorts of experiments with new ways of being church plus emerging churches of all sorts. The original *Mission-shaped Church* report and Fresh Expressions were endorsed and developed[45] and also criticized from many angles.[46] Some of the concerns were, first, that mission studies is in danger of being reduced to social and cultural anthropology without its ethical, historical, and theological dimensions; second, that the mission-shaped church approach may lead to multiplying churches to compete for "customers" in a way that is contrary to the spirit of Christian unity, or to the "McDonaldization" of the gospel and the church for the sake of the efficiency, calculability, predictability, and control so valued in the market;[47] and third, that the original report assumed a homogenous English culture and paid little attention to ethnic minorities or to social inequality, both of which are issues that a rounded study of mission should include. However the report did help to establish is the missionary nature of the local church and ensured that mission studies is represented in this way in most places where training for ministry takes place.

Mission and culture

Despite criticism of mission-shaped church, attention to the relationship of mission and culture continued, and probably the chief dialogue partners of mission studies in 2012 were cultural studies and postcolonial thought. This dialogue resulted in a variety of different

45   E.g. Gray Cray, Ian Mobsby and Aaron Kennedy, *New Monasticism as Fresh Expression of Church* (Norwich: Canterbury Press, 2010); Steven Croft and Ian Mobsby, *Fresh Expressions in the Sacramental Tradition* (Norwich: Canterbury Press, 2009); Steven Croft, *Mission-shaped Questions: Defining Issues for Today's Church* (London: Church House Publishing, 2008); Paul Bayes, Tim Sledge, John Holbrook, Mark Rylands, Martin Seeley, *Mission-shaped Parish: Traditional Church in a Changing World* (London: Church House Publishing, 2009).

46   E.g. John Hull, *Mission-shaped Church: A Theological Response* (London: SCM, 2006); Andrew Davison and Alison Milbank, *For the Parish: A Critique of Fresh Expressions* (London: SCM, 2010). Martyn Percy and Louise Nelstrop, *Evaluating Fresh Expressions: Explorations in Emerging Church* (Norwich: Canterbury Press, 2008).

47   John Drane, *The McDonaldization of the Church: Spirituality, Creativity, and the Future of the Church* (London: Darton, Longman and Todd, 2000).

approaches. Most of these were represented in the wide-ranging lecture series of the Oxford Centre for Christianity and Culture at Regent's Park College. At the University of Birmingham many mission-related studies were carried out under the heading "intercultural studies"[48] or using the post-colonial approaches pioneered by R.S. Sugirtharajah at Selly Oak and the University of Birmingham. Black theology was represented by Anthony Reddie, then at the Queen's Foundation, Birmingham.[49] Gordon Lynch, at the University of Kent, looked at the interface of religion with postmodern and popular culture.[50] David Kettle, who led the Gospel and Our Culture Network, built on the work of Lesslie Newbigin to challenge Western culture in general. Anne Richards led the Mission Theological Advisory Group of the Church of England and Churches Together to take postmodern and popular culture seriously and approach them sympathetically through contact points with spirituality.[51] After the attention given to Celtic spirituality in the 1980s and 90s,[52] recent missional attention was being given English culture. Christianity and Culture, directed by Dee Dyas of St John's Nottingham and the University

---

48   E.g. Mark J. Cartledge and David Cheetham (eds), *Intercultural Theology: A Primer* (London: SCM Press, 2011).

49   More recently brought together in Anthony Reddie, *Black Theology*. SCM Core Text (London: SCM Press, 2012).

50   Gordon Lynch, *Understanding Theology and Popular Culture* (Oxford: Blackwell, 2005).

51   See www.spiritualjourneys.org.uk and Anne Richards (ed.), *Sense Making Faith: Body, Spirit, Journey* (London: Churches Together In Britain and Ireland, 2008).

52   E.g. Esther de Waal, *Every Earthly Blessing: Rediscovering the Celtic Tradition* (London: Fount, 1991) and the papers of the BIAMS conference in Maynooth, Ireland, in 1997 on Columba versus Augustine, *BIAMS Newsletter* 9 (Sept. 1997).

of York, explored the influence of Christianity in English culture through history.[53] Nigel Rooms from Nottingham looked at contemporary English culture with a view to integrating, or re-integrating, the gospel with it.[54]

Mission spirituality and pneumatology

At the turn of the millennium, spirituality and mission was a current area of interest in BIAMS.[55] In 2004 the results of a major research project led by Paul Heelas and Linda Woodhead at Lancaster University caused a stir in the press when they showed there was a shift from "religion" to "spirituality"; that is, away from belief in a system expressed through membership of a congregation and toward individual pursuit of subjective experience especially through alternative "holistic," therapeutic religious experience of a neo-Pagan or New Age type.[56] Some Fresh Expressions and other creative ways of being church were included in the Heelas-Woodhead definition of spirituality.[57] Steve Hollinghurst at the Sheffield Centre was

---

53   E.g. Dee Dyas, *The Bible in Western Culture: The Student's Guide* (Abingdon: Routledge, 2005).

54   Nigel Rooms, *The Faith of the English: Integrating Christ and Culture* (London: SPCK, 2011).

55   The BIAMS day conference in September 2000 considered "The Spirituality of the Un-Churched" led by David Hay and this led into the 2001 residential BIAMS conference, published as Howard Mellor and Timothy Yates *Mission and Spirituality: Creative Ways of Being Church* (Sheffield: Cliff College Publishing, 2002).

56   The Kendal Project, www.kendalproject.org.uk; Paul Heelas and Linda Woodhead, *The Spiritual Revolution: Why Religion is Giving Way to Spirituality* (Oxford: Blackwell 2004).

57   "Fresh Expressions", see www.freshexpressions.org.uk; See also The Group for Evangelisation (Churches Together in England), "Church in a Spiritual Age", at www.churchinaspiritualage.org.uk and Steve Hollinghurst, Yvonne Richmond and Roger Whitehead, with Janice Price and Tina Adams, *Equipping Your Church in a Spiritual Age* (London: Church House Publishing, 2005).

doing mission studies in relation to such post-Christian groups.[58] Since, holistic spiritualities involve a new relationship to the creation and the natural world, eco-theologies and a mission of environmental justice were being developed, particularly by Celia Deane-Drummond, then at the University of Chester, and David Bookless of A Rocha, who both spoke at the BIAMS day conference in 2007.[59]

Interest in God in creation and in spiritual experience and spirituality were two reasons for increased attention to the Holy Spirit and to pneumatological perspectives in mission studies. Another reason is the rise of Pentecostal and charismatic perspectives in the study of mission, culture, and practical theology. The latter was reflected particularly at the Centre for Pentecostal and Charismatic Studies, University of Birmingham and in the work of Allan Anderson, Mark Cartledge, and Andrew Smith there. A noticeable shift had taken place in the *missio Dei* paradigm, which was first expressed as "partnership in Christ" but which had now become "finding out where the Holy Spirit is at work and joining in".[60] As Andrew Lord explained, holistic mission is "Spirit-shaped mission".[61]

Mission, evangelism and other faiths

Although the growing presence of non-Christian faiths had provided impetus for the establishment of BIAMS, most Christian involvement with them was now separated from mission studies under the heading

58 Steve Hollinghurst, *Mission Shaped Evangelism: The Gospel in Contemporary Culture* (Norwich: Canterbury Press, 2010).

59 See, Celia Deane-Drummond, *Eco-theology* (London: Darton, Longman and Todd, 2008); David Bookless, *Planetwise* (Leicester: Inter Varsity Press, 2008), also *Mission Studies* 25/1 (2008).

60 Rowan Williams – quoted on the Fresh Expressions website, www. freshexpressions.org.uk, front page (Sept 2006); Kirsteen Kim, *Joining in with the Spirit: Connecting World Church and Local Mission* (Peterborough: Epworth, 2009; London: SCM Press, 2012).

61 Andrew Lord, *Spirit-shaped Mission: A Holistic Charismatic Missiology* (Milton Keynes: Paternoster, 2005). Many of the implications of this shift are captured in the recent World Council of Churches' statement *Together towards Life: Mission and Evangelism in Changing Landscapes* (2013). Available from

of interfaith or dialogue. However, after 9/11 and 7/7 called government policy of multi-culturalism into question, there developed a more robust dialogue and it was recognized that prophesy and proclamation—from all sides—has a place in inter-religious relations.[62] A Church of England report in 2005 advocated a closer relationship between mission, evangelism and dialogue through Presence and Engagement.[63] There was growing recognition that religions may be in mission toward one another[64] and in a new willingness to learn from the long experience of many churches outside the West, who have lived as minorities in nations dominated by other faiths, about how to engage with different religions.[65]

Mission and economic justice

In the post-colonial era the work done by missionary societies in education, medical care and other aspects of human well-being, which was such a large part of their work before the Second World War, was mostly transferred to governments, development agencies and other secular bodies. In the secularist environment since then, Christian mission organizations which engage in development activities were sometimes tarred with suspicion that they may be using this as a cover for church

---

www.wcc-coe.org. See also Kim, *Joining in with the Spirit*.

62   Israel Selvanayagam, then principal of the United College of the Ascension, drawing on his Indian experience, always insisted that evangelism and dialogue were inseparable. E.g. Israel Selvanayagam, *A Second Call: Ministry and Mission in a Multifaith Milieu* (Madras: CLS, 2000), 338-53.

63   See website, http://presenceandengagement.org.uk/.

64   See, the seminal article written in 2000 by David A. Kerr, then professor of Christianity in the non-Western world at the University of Edinburgh, which compared Islamic Da'wa and Christian mission: David A. Kerr, "Islamic *Da'wa* and Christian Mission: Towards a Comparative Analysis", *International Review of Mission* 89/353, pp. 150-171. See also, the results of the Lambeth-Jewish Forum, Reuven Silverman, Patrick Morrow and Daniel Langton, *Jews and Christians: Perspectives on Mission* (Lambeth-Jewish Forum, 2010). Available at www.woolf.cam.ac.uk.

65   E.g. Heythrop College and CTBI jointly hosted a colloquium in 2011 on "Globalised Christianity and Inter Faith Engagement: Implications for Theological Reflection in Britain and Ireland" at Heythrop College.

expansion or inducing people to convert for ulterior motives. In such a climate it was a struggle to maintain a holistic approach in mission. But the first decade of the twenty-first century witnessed something of a change in attitude as represented, for example, by the Religions and Development project of the International Development Department of the University of Birmingham, which was funded by the government Department for International Development to explore "the relationships between several major world religions, development in low-income countries and poverty reduction."[66] The project showed the extent to which, in the Christian case, mission agencies and churches themselves are agents of development and it encouraged a partnership of faith-based organizations with government bodies. Similarly within the UK, successive governments encouraged faith-based social initiatives for a number of political reasons. In view of mission history, mission studies has a critical role to play vis-à-vis such policies. In the Jubilee 2000 and Make Poverty History (2005) campaigns, the UK led the world in this respect as mission organizations and development agencies came together with churches and faith groups to exert considerable political pressure on the world's political leaders meeting as the G8 to address questions of debt and poverty. In view of the current economic crisis, I argued, it was more necessary than ever that mission studies address itself to questions of economic justice.

Mission, public theology, and reconciliation

In first decade of the twenty-first century "public theology" emerged as a missional interface with public affairs, politics, and civil society: "Public theology is an engagement of living religious traditions with their public environment—the economic, political and cultural spheres of common life".[67] The Global Network for Public Theology included a disproportionate number of institutions and centers in the UK.[68]

---

66   See www.religionsanddevelopment.org.

67   Sebastian C.H. Kim, Editorial, *International Journal of Public Theology*, 1/1 (2007), 1-4 (p. 2).

68   Centre for the Study of Religion and Politics, University of St Andrews; Centre for Theology and Public Issues, University of Edinburgh; Irish School of Ecumenics, Trinity College Dublin; Manchester Centre for Public Theology, University of Manchester; University of Exeter Network for

There were also specialist institutions, such as the London Institute for Contemporary Christianity and the Kirby Laing Institute for Christian Ethics, Cambridge and a number of Christian public theology think-tanks such as Theos and Ekklesia, which aimed to bring theology to public life. Public theology is less adversarial than the political theology which arose in the 1960s or the liberation theologies of the 1970s and 1980s. One of the main contributions of theology in the public sphere was to work for reconciliation in society on the basis of the reconciliation in Christ. Reflection on mission as reconciliation was particularly developed in Ireland by theologians from different communities.[69] It was the subject of the BIAMS conference in Belfast in 2003.[70] Reconciliation was the focus of a conference at York St. John University (which is part of an ongoing worldwide series) and a series of seminars at the United College of the Ascension.[71]

Mission and migration

The Wallsian "shift in the center of gravity of Christianity" heightened the importance of dialogue with theologies from Africa, Asia, and Latin America but still this tended to be treated as an exotic optional extra in theological studies. In the past decade such dialogue had become less of a choice as more and more churches from the global south and east migrated to the UK. The relevance of studies of migration to mission studies was recognized particularly by Afe Adogame at the University of Edinburgh

Religion and Public Life; and York St. John University. Luke Bretherton also made an important contribution at King's College London: Luke Bretherton, *Christianity and Contemporary Politics: The Conditions and Possibilities of Faithful Witness* (Wiley-Blackwell, 2010).

69 Notably through the Irish School of Ecumenics at Trinity College, Dublin. See, e.g., Joseph Liechty and Cecelia Clegg, *Moving Beyond Sectarianism: Religion, Conflict and Reconciliation in Northern Ireland* (Blackrock: Columba Press, 2001).

70 Howard Mellor and Timothy Yates (eds.), *Mission, Violence and Reconciliation* (Sheffield: Cliff College Publishing, 2004).

71 Sebastian C.H. Kim, Pauline Kollontai and Greg Hoyland (eds), *Peace and Reconciliation: In Search of Shared Identity* (Aldershot: Ashgate, 2008); Kirsteen Kim (ed.), *Reconciling Mission: The Ministry of Healing and Reconciliation in the Church Worldwide* (Delhi: SPCK, 2005).

and Emma Wild-Wood in Cambridge, and BIAMS focused on this at its conference in 2007.[72] I pointed out that in a globalized world what is going on "out there" cannot be ignored because sooner or later it will also be here and therefore "world church and local mission" need to be more closely connected.[73] The greatest blind-spot in mission studies has always been reflection on the West as part of the global community, and this is a legacy of colonialism. The mission-shaped church debate, for example, failed to recognize the "migrant churches" that would be identified just a few years later as important examples of new and emerging churches. Since the end of the colonial period, Europe has also been recognized as a mission field and it is now being treated as such not only by North Americans but also by the agents of what has been termed "reverse mission".[74] I concluded that mission studies needed to do more to interface with global or international affairs in order to understand the global significance of mission movements and their local implications for churches. Above all, understanding the United States, its impact on the world and these nations in particular, and its influence on our practice of Christianity, should be an important part of mission studies. The reflections of migrants and reverse missionaries, who see Britain and Ireland from outsider perspectives, enriches mission studies by setting the discourse within a wider context and helping us to see ourselves as others do.[75]

Further Developments in Mission Studies (2015)

In the three years since 2012, there have been further significant changes in the landscape of mission studies. As we increasingly see ourselves in contemporary Britain and Ireland as in a missional context, insights from mission studies have become more relevant and have permeated the rest of

---

72   Afe Adogame, *Christianity in Africa and the African Diaspora* (London: Continuum, 2011); Emma Wild-Wood, *Migration and Christian Identity in Congo* (Leiden: Brill, 2008). Papers of the BIAMS conference of 2007 are published as Stephen Spencer (ed.), *Mission and Migration* (Sheffield: Cliff College Publishing, 2008).

73   Kim, *Joining in with the Spirit*.

74   E.g. Rebecca Catto, "Non-Western Christian Missionaries in England: Has Mission Been Reversed?", *BIAMS Bulletin* 30 (March 2008), pp. 2-9.

75   There are many reflective papers on mission in the UK from outsider perspectives posted on the *Rethinking Mission* website created by USPG, www.rethinkingmission.org.uk

the theological curriculum.[76] However, alongside a decline in institutional church life, the study of academic theology of any kind has continued a long decline. This is most marked at undergraduate level; postgraduate numbers are more resilient. This has affected interest in mission studies in two main ways: first, it is a victim of its own success in that mission is no longer distinguishable from other church activities; second, the shift of interest in mission to the local church has tended to benefit the study of practical theology rather than mission studies. The effect of both activities combined was that, in 2014, BIAMS accepted an invitation to become a network within the British and Irish Association for Practical Theology (BIAPT) and ceased to exist as a separate entity. So where does that leave missiology in Britain and Ireland? I have shown that the permeation of aspects of mission studies in theological studies is greater than ever before but the focused study of mission, particularly in its global dimensions, is struggling. In this situation, I suggest two further ways in which interest in mission studies can be maintained and re-ignited: missiology as theology for world Christianity and missiology as the study of evangelization.

Missiology as theology for world Christianity

Given the continued interest in "world Christianity," while continuing to develop as "mission studies" or "missiology," mission studies should today claim to the name "theology for world Christianity." I concluded the 2012 article with a plea that studies of mission and world Christianity would continue to enhance and diversify the theological curriculum leading to its genuine internalization so that it reflects the reality of our nations and that Britain and Ireland are part of world Christianity. The shift in the center of Christianity away from Europe is changing the churches in Britain and Ireland. This is seen, for example, by the way the shape and authority structures of the Anglican Communion have been challenged on issues of human sexuality, for example by the church in Nigeria, which has significantly more practicing Christians than the English church.[77] The presence of so many "migrant churches" in these islands is also a challenge to assumptions that there is a normative form of Christianity here, which

---

76   Kim, *Joining in with the Spirit*.

77   For insight into the issues, see Terry Brown (ed), *Other Voices, Other Worlds: The Global Church Speaks Out on Homosexuality* (London: Darton, Longman and Todd, 2006).

is also a global norm, and to which newcomers need to be assimilated. The evidence that we are part of world Christianity should make an impact on theological education which is both profound and broad. We can no longer assume that our students were formed here or that their ministry will be to a settled population originating in these nations and sharing the same culture (if that assumption was ever true). We have a multi-cultural Christian community which is in touch with, and open to, global trends in theology and practice.

The rise in interest in world Christianity attests to a growing awareness of the importance of global perspectives and recognition of the interconnectedness of Christian movements across the world. Philip Jenkins, another influential (originally) British scholar in the field, drew attention to the significance of this for theology when he wrote: "All too often statements about what 'modern Christians accept' or 'what Catholics today believe' refer only to what that ever-shrinking remnant of *Western* Christians and Catholics believe. Such assertions are outrageous today, and as time goes by they will become ever further removed from reality."[78] We do not yet see in Britain and Ireland significant change in the teaching of theology, although Regnum Books International has been responding to this challenge for several years.[79] It should be the case that practical theology takes account of global affairs; biblical studies interfaces with cultural, postcolonial, and religious studies; church history recognizes simultaneous histories of different regions of the world; and dogmatic or systematic theology engages African, Asian, and Indigenous philosophies and theologies. The church is moving in migration and mission and so theology also needs to move beyond recounting and developing the Western tradition toward much greater engagement with theologies emerging from other contexts. Missiology, by its nature, has important resources to inform the debate about how the teaching of theology responds to these challenges. It can facilitate the internationalization of theology and global theological conversation.[80]

---

78   Philip Jenkins, *The Next Christendom* (Oxford: OUP, 2002), 3.

79   Regnum Books International publishes on mission, global Christianity, resources for mission and also includes the Regnum Edinburgh Centenary Series. See www.ocms.org.uk/regnum.

80   Kirsteen Kim, *The Holy Spirit in the World: A Global Conversation* (Maryknoll, NY: Orbis Books / London: SPCK, 2007).

Missiology as the study of evangelization

The *missio Dei* paradigm, in which all human missions are thought of as part of the one mission of God, has formed the theological foundation for ecumenical mission studies since the 1950s.[81] It was given its fullest development in David Bosch's work, *Transforming Mission*. However, there is increasing theological and missiological discontent with the "paradigm" of *missio Dei*. The extension of *missio Dei* to suggest that God's work in the world might bypass the church was challenged by Bosch.[82] Furthermore, much *missio Dei* theology is a form of the social Trinity, a model which has been heavily criticized as ideologically constructed.[83] The World Council of Churches' statement *Together towards Life* overcame the separation of the immanent and economic Trinity in *missio Dei* formulations by focusing instead on the mission of the Spirit. Missiologically, the *missio Dei* paradigm was established in the very different context of the Cold War as a way of responding to the limitations on horizontal sending in that era and it was developed in the 1960s to justify mission as a secular development movement.[84] It has encouraged biblical reflection on mission and conception of the church as missional.[85] But it also implicitly

---

81 John Paul II, *Redemptoris Missio*: On the Permanent Validity of the Church's Missionary Mandate (1990; available at www.vatican.va); Lausanne Movement, The Cape Town Commitment (2011; available at www.lausanne. org).

82 Bosch, *Transforming Mission*, 381-89.

83 E.g. Kathryn Tanner, "Trinity", in Scott and Cavanaugh, *Political Theology* (Oxford: Blackwell, 2007), 319-32. John Flett's recent corrective of the tendency of *missio Dei* theology to cleave God's being from his act goes a long way to responding to Tanner's criticism by reconnecting the *missio Dei* to the kingdom of God. John G. Flett, *The Witness of God: The Trinity, Missio Dei, Karl Barth, and the Nature of Christian Community* (Grand Rapids, MI: Wm B. Eerdmans, 2010), 290-92.

84 For in-depth study of the origins of the *missio Dei* paradigm, see Flett, *The Witness of God*.

85 Stanley H. Skreslet, *Comprehending Mission: The Questions, Methods, Themes, Problems, and Prospects of Missiology* (Maryknoll, NY: Orbis Books, 2012), 31-33.

discourages horizontal or geographical sending. Moreover, *missio Dei* has been appealed to for so many causes as to render Bosch's "consensus" largely meaningless.

Since at least Edinburgh 1910, an alternative and often synonymous term to mission has been "evangelization." From a biblical studies perspective, evangelization—"proclaiming" or "effecting" good news— could be regarded as the Lukan version (Luke 4 : 18) of the Johannine mission—"sending" (John 3 : 16; 20 : 21). Whereas mission theology starts from above with the sending of Christ, evangelization starts from below by following the example of Jesus Christ. Long before the shift away from "missions" as activities of the church to "mission" to refer to God's sending, Protestants in 1910 used evangelization in a holistic way. In 1975, Pope Paul VI in *Evangelii Nuntiandi* adopted this term to describe a broad missional agenda[86] and in 2013 Pope Francis revived its use in *Evangelii Gaudium*, also in a broad sense that covers most of what is discussed under mission in Protestant circles.[87] The publication of *Evangelii Gaudium* presents an opportunity to bring the two parts of the Western church together for renewed discussion on mission under the heading of evangelization. Furthermore, since the term "gospel" is embedded in it,[88] use of evangelization helps to identify the Christian agenda in an era when "mission" is used by all sorts of organizations, businesses, and so on. Certainly in the UK *Evangelii Gaudium* has awakened interest in mission themes.[89]

---

86 *Evangelii Nuntiandi*. Apostolic Exhortation of Paul VI following the third assembly of the Synod of Bishops in 1974 (1975; available from www.vatican.va).

87 And more besides because it included pastoral ministry. *Evangelii Gaudium*. Apostolic Exhortation of Francis on "The Proclamation of the Gospel in Today's World" (2013; available at www.vatican.va). The exhortation followed the thirteenth assembly of the Synod of Bishops, which had been organised by Benedict XVI in 2012 on "The New Evangelization". See Paul Grogan and Kirsteen Kim (eds), *The New Evangelization: Faith, People, Context and Practice* (London: Bloomsbury T & T Clark, 2015).

88 I concede that the connection with "good news" is lost on most English speakers but it is more obvious in other languages.

89 E.g. the conference, "'Making all things new'? *Evangelii Gaudium* and Ecumenical Mission", St. John's College, Cambridge, 29 June—1 July 2015. See http://evangeliigaudium.co.uk/.

In conclusion, although study of mission as a discipline in its own right has declined in the UK and Ireland since 2000, the themes and insights of mission studies are increasingly found in ministerial training and in studies of world Christianity. They have the potential to internationalize theology, but this is not yet realized, and there is an opportunity to revive mission as evangelization. The term "mission" is popular in the churches but may be toxic in academic settings. The challenge is, on the one hand, to keep ministerial training in touch with developments in the academy and the wider world and, on the other, to maintain relationships between the study of religion at secular universities and what actually happens in churches. In other words, it is to hold together the study of local mission or evangelization and research on world Christianity and theology worldwide.

From Mcgavran's Church Growth to Taber's Kingdom of God

Tracing Distinct Missiological Trajectories
in Undergraduate and Graduate Mission and
Intercultural Studies Programs in Christian
Churches/ Churches of Christ Instiutions

KEVIN (KIP) LINES, PHD

DOI: 10.7252/Paper. 000052

About the Author
Kevin (Kip) Lines (PhD, Asbury Theological Seminary), currently serves as
Associate Professor of Intercultural Studies at Hope International University in
Fullerton, CA. Before serving as a missionary alongside Turkana church leaders in
Turkana, Kenya with CMF International (1999-2008), he completed his graduate
degree at Emmanuel School of Religion. He was one of the last graduates to study
under Charles Taber before his retirement in 1998.

Abstract:

Two of the most influential and well-known missiologists with connections to the Christian Churches/Churches of Christ, Donald A. McGavran (1897-1990) and Charles R. Taber (1928-2007), had distinctly different approaches toward missiology and its application in the academic setting. While McGavran's approach led to very formalized missiological programs, eventually at Fuller Theological Seminary, Taber suggested that missiology should not be a separate subject in the seminary curriculum, but should instead be an integral part of every course of study. This paper compares current missiological and intercultural studies undergraduate and graduate programs in 20 Christian Churches/Churches of Christ institutions, and views them through these two missiological models. This comparison provides a framework for understanding varied approaches in different institutions (even outside of the American Stone-Campbell Christian Church movement).

Introduction of my own Missiological Lenses

This paper is a combination of both long-standing and recent personal endeavors. As one of Dr. Charles Taber's last graduate students before his retirement in 1998, I have carried with me many insights gleaned from a man who was better known in missiological and linguistic circles than those of us who attended a small east Tennessee seminary realized. Taber challenged me as a seminary student to consider why I felt called to serve as a missionary in Kenya, a country from which church leaders, most notably John Gatu, had called for a moratorium on all western missionaries and funding in 1971. This was 25 years before my calling to serve as a missionary in Kenya. Taber wanted me to squarely confront the dichotomy of my calling, together with the moratorium debates, encouraging me to critically examine the history of the mission moratorium for my Master's thesis; a task that I undertook and will forever be grateful for (Lines 1998). Taber was not opposed to western missionaries in Africa, but was rightly concerned that "the sending of western Missionaries to open new fields ought not to be an automatic reflex, nor ought it to take place at all without an accompanying effort to establish close and cordial relations with national churches" (Taber 1973:3). It was with that knowledge that I served as a missionary alongside my wife and local church leaders in Turkana, Kenya from 1999-2008.

After returning from missionary service, in my first semester of PhD coursework at Asbury Theological Seminary, while studying contextual theology under the tutelage of Dr. Eunice Erwin, I was surprised that required reading included articles authored by Taber. Certainly this wasn't the Taber I studied under at Emmanuel School of Religion, whose funeral I had just attended while on furlough in 2007? It was. At that point, I began to collect and read all of the writings of Dr. Taber and worked with archivists at both Milligan College and Emmanuel Christian Seminary to gain copies of his unpublished works and presentations. My wife and I even visited with and interviewed Taber's wife, Betty, who remains active in her church community in Johnson City, TN.

It was Taber who introduced me to Church Growth and Donald A. McGavran, in a course titled "The Biblical Basis of Church Growth," in which students were required to read McGavran's *Understanding Church Growth* and then listen to lectures in which Taber skillfully dismantled McGavran's writing, often point by point, with careful biblical exegesis. He expected that we learn Church Growth theory, but he taught us that the kingdom of God was not limited by church growth principles.

Yet my ministry experience as a missionary with CMF International was very positively influenced by Donald A. McGavran's church growth theories. The CMFI mission organization emerged from the American Christian Church unity movement (also known as the Stone-Campbell Movement) that placed a high value on mission and evangelism. The unity that the movement was founded on was not seen as an end in itself, but was to enhance Christian witness to non-Christians. Writing in 1824, Alexander Campbell made clear his concern that, without unity among Christians, our efforts in "conversion of the world" would be in vain (*Christian Baptist*, 2:135, 1824). He was convinced that division among Christians would be the greatest stumbling block to non-Christians accepting Jesus as Lord (*Christian Baptist*, 1:40-42, 1824). Our unity as Christians within individual congregations, without sectarian and denominational divisions, could be a key strategy in our evangelistic mission. This affirms Jesus' earnest prayer for the Church in John 17; not merely for a unity in the Church so we could all coexist, but "so that the world may believe" (John 17:21).

The Stone-Campbell Movement Churches were among the early leaders in the modern Protestant missionary movement in America. As congregations were sending out missionaries, churches gathered to form a cooperative mission sending organization in 1849, the American Christian Missionary Society (later, the Foreign Christian Missionary Society), in which more than 100 representatives from 100 Stone-Campbell Movement churches worked together to send missionary James Barclay to Jerusalem (Blowers 2004). These churches were also leaders in the formation of the Christian Women's Board of Missions, during an era when women missionaries outnumbered male missionaries almost 2:1.

McGavran's father taught at the Indianapolis College of Missions, which was founded by women leaders in Stone-Campbell Movement congregations in 1909. This school moved and later became the Kennedy School of Missions at Hartford Seminary in Hartford, Connecticut. As expected from a Christian unity movement, representatives from both of these Stone-Campbell mission boards (the ACMS and CWBM) were present at the influential 1910 World Missionary Conference in Edinburgh, Scotland, including 12-year-old Donald McGavran. McGavran attended with his parents, and would later serve as a 3rd generation Stone-Campbell missionary with the United Christian Mission Society in India, after earning a graduate degree at the College of Mission in Indianapolis.

After returning from two terms in India, McGavran received his PhD from Columbia University and became one of the leading missiologists of the 20th century, utilizing the application of the social sciences for mission and founding a graduate theological school devoted to church growth and evangelism at Northwest Christian College. This original Church Growth Institute met around a large oak table on the 3rd floor of the library at Northwest Christian College. Early CMFI missionaries were among the first students at the Institute. Many of them were the missionaries who preceded me and set up the mission structures and methods CMFI used in East Africa (McGavran 1986).

After McGavran was invited to move his Institute to Fuller in 1965 and serve as the founding dean of the School of World Mission, CMFI missionaries were required to complete their graduate studies at Fuller for field preparation as early as 1967. Even later, as CMFI policy was relaxed and a Master's degree from Fuller was not required for field service, the East African CMFI teams still required new recruits to take 5 core graduate level classes from Fuller: church growth, language acquisition, cultural anthropology, theology of mission, and folk religion.

Further relaxing of the policy eventually allowed recruits to take the 5 core graduate classes anywhere they wanted, but a Church Growth class was still required. Highlighting the tension in the missiological perspectives of McGavran and Taber, special permission was required from the leadership of CMFI for my wife and I to receive these five core courses from Taber at Emmanuel Christian Seminary. An outspoken critic of McGavran, Taber took opportunities, even in book reviews, to critique what he considered McGavran's straw man arguments, superficiality, "theological and biblical foundations [that] remain casual, superficial and anecdotal rather than profound and intrinsic," and "quite insubstantial empirical foundations" (Taber 1986).

Still, beyond Taber's critiques of McGavran during my seminary training, McGavran had a direct positive (dare I say *effective*) influence on the CMFI ministries we joined in East Africa. McGavran visited Ethiopia in 1972 to lead a Church Growth seminar in Addis Ababa and then visited with the CMF team working in southern and western Ethiopia in Tosse. At the seminar in Addis, O.D. Johnson, the first general director of CMFI, presented the paper, "A Mission Founded on Church Growth Principles." While in Tosse, McGavran presented a church growth seminar to the Ethiopian church leaders and then met with the CMFI missionaries, encouraging them to "create strategies that would bring a harvest of all of the peoples to Christ in the areas where they were working" (Chapman 2015).

When all Protestant missionaries were expelled from Ethiopia in 1977, many of the CMFI missionaries moved to Kenya to begin new work among the unreached, yet receptive, Maasai and Turkana peoples. The initial survey of the far northern Turkana district in Kenya was carried out with church growth principles and social scientific research methods, focused on the potential receptivity of the Turkana people (Elliston 1979).

The extended introduction to this paper highlights the reasoning behind my inquiry and my interwoven connections with the Stone-Campbell movement, Donald A. McGavran, Charles R. Taber, the application of church growth principles in an intercultural ministry context, and as the lead professor in an undergraduate intercultural studies program. This is a complicated set of lenses, but a set that uniquely affects my own missiological vision. As I began to examine the missions/ICS programs in the 20 independent Christian Church institutions in my study, this was the set of lenses through which I examined them.

McGavran and Taber: Visions for Missiological Education

Donald A. McGavran (1897-1990)

While a biographical sketch of McGavran has already been provided, I would like to emphasize a few key features of McGavran's missiological vision and the way this was played out in an educational model.

It must be noted that McGavran's vision was heavily influenced by Roland Allen's earlier reflections on the errors of modern missions based on his experiences in China and the experiences and reflections of J. Waskom Pickett, a fellow missionary in India. From Allen's perspective, the spontaneous expansion of Christianity was being stifled by the methods of modern missions, especially the mission compound model. McGavran's response was to emphasize "a new kind of strategizing that incorporated a sociological perspective" (Skreslet 2012:141). This included focusing mission efforts where there was a greater possibility for numerical success.

McGavran described the basis for his vision as a conviction that "God wants his lost children found and enfolded" (McGavran 1986:57). From this conviction came an essential component for church growth thinking: research must be carried out to discover the facts of growth in missionary planted churches around the world. It is then with these facts that mission leaders and missionaries could engage in "planning all mission activities in the light of what is being achieved" (McGavran 1986:58).

It was McGavran that brought serious research back to Christian mission. When McGavran was young and attended the College of Missions in Indianapolis, George Hunter III describes a situation in which,

> mission was taught in virtually every seminary curriculum, and there were schools of mission and prominent graduate programs. In the 1950s, 1960s, and much of the 1970s, under the impact of theological liberalism, religious intolerance, and other Enlightenment influences, schools of mission expired while, in seminaries, retiring missions professors were not replaced and mission dropped out of the curriculum. (Hunter 1992:159)

This trend was reversed by McGavran's influence through the School of World Mission at Fuller. Through his models and writings, mission again became part of the curriculum of many independent colleges and seminaries.

McGavran's educational model was fully set in motion when he was invited by President Hubbard at Fuller Theological Seminary to become the founding dean of the School of World Mission in 1965. McGavran recounts that these were the best years of his pilgrimage, as he engaged in the task of "recruit[ing] seven full-time professors and making this graduate school serve the missionary cause around the world" (McGavran 1986:57). Additionally, this model "multiplied amazingly in many lands" and "other schools of mission borrowed extensively" from the church growth research and training model.

The School of World Mission became a new model for missiological education in a number of ways. First, it was a separate school and faculty from the school of theology. While in the older institutions missiology was viewed as part of theology, or even by some as the "mother of theology" (e.g. Martin Kähler, cited in Bosch 1991:16), in this new model the schools of theology/biblical studies and missiology were now separate specialized schools with distinct programs. A second new approach was gathering faculty specialists in church growth, communication theory, anthropology, folk religion, language acquisition, evangelism, mission history, mission spirituality, mission theology and contextual theologies. Through the gathering of specialists, missiology truly became an interdisciplinary field of study. A third new emphasis of this model was to gather missiological research through the training of students in qualitative and quantitative social science research methods.

Charles R. Taber (1928-2007)

Born to American Brethren missionaries training in Paris, Taber resided in France the first eight years of his life and was afforded one of the preeminent advantages of a Third Culture Kid: being bilingual from birth. After a one-year furlough in the States, Taber then lived with his parents in the French colony of Oubangui-Chari, which is now known as the Central African Republic, where for five years they resided and young Taber learned to speak the Sango language from other children. During World War II, the family moved to South Africa for 6 months, then to Southern Rhodesia for 3 months, before briefly returning to Oubangui-Chari. While in South Africa, Taber notes that he began his first year of high school in English. After returning to the U.S., Taber remained to finish his last two years of high school in Allentown, Pennsylvania (Taber 2005:89).

There is no doubt these early experiences helped to form an understanding of language that would serve Taber well the rest of his life as a missionary in the Central African Republic, as a linguist with the United Bible Societies in West Africa, and later, as a professor of world mission. Fluency in multiple languages helped Taber become one of the foremost Bible translation experts, providing direction for innumerable translation projects through *The Theory and Practice of Translation*, co-authored with Eugene Nida in 1969. This text was reprinted as recently as 2003 in English and translated into multiple languages, most recently into Mandarin and published in Shanghai in 2004.

Majoring in English while teaching French as an undergraduate at Bryan College, Taber met his wife, Betty, and the two were married the summer after graduation in 1951. They served together as missionaries in the Central African Republic with the Foreign Missionary Society of the Brethren church from 1953 until about 1960. After returning to the States to care for family medical issues, Taber was invited by his former Oubangui-Chari colleague, William Samarin, to pursue graduate studies at the Kennedy School of Missions at the Hartford Seminary Foundation. Taber immediately accepted the invitation. Samarin and Taber would later publish *A Dictionary of Sango* in 1964 (Taber 2005:90).

Robert J. Priest has noted that many prominent Christian linguists and anthropologists attended the Kennedy School of Missions at Hartford Seminary during this time period, as it was the only place for doctoral work in missiology in the decades following Edinburgh 1910. This mainline Protestant school,

> fielded a faculty of noted linguists, comparative religionists, sociologists (such as Peter Berger), and anthropologists (Absalom Vilakazi, Paul Leser, Morris Steggerda, Edwin Smith). George Peters, Charles Kraft, Dean Gilliland, and Charles Taber were among those who received doctorates here. (Robert J. Priest, *Christianity Today, 10/1/2007* "Paul Hiebert: A Life Remembered")

Taber completed an M.A. in 1964, a Ph.D. in 1966, and had begun working with Eugene Nida of the American Bible Society before graduating from Hartford Seminary.

Serving from 1969-1973 as a United Bible Societies translation consultant who provided oversight for more than two dozen projects in West Africa, Taber simultaneously served as the editor of the journal *Practical Anthropology* for the four years previous to its merging with *Missiology* in 1973. After completing a term with the UBS, Taber was invited by Tetsunao Yamamori to help start an institute of world mission and church growth at Milligan College, Tennessee. After six years of teaching at the undergraduate level in which he felt he was not well suited, Yamamori leaving to take another position elsewhere, and the mission institute at Milligan College never materializing for lack of finances, Taber began teaching at Emmanuel School of Religion, a graduate seminary that served the Christian churches/churches of Christ, in 1979, where he taught for 18 years. During this time he served as the president of the Association of Professors of Mission in 1981, the president of the American Society of Missiology in 1985-86 and as an ASM Publication Series Editor from 1988-1997 (Taber 2005:92).

In his autobiographical reflection, Taber noted a few major realizations through the years that will help us understand his missiological vision. First, while working with the UBS in West Africa, he and Betty "came to realize as never before that the Bible does not need to be protected by a nineteenth-century philosophical scaffold; it just needs to be turned loose" (Taber 2005:92). For Taber, this meant that the Scriptures did not require the incessant interpretations of missionaries or translators. While Taber held a very high view of Scripture, he came to understand that the "national church was capable of being guided by the Holy Spirit using the Scriptures" (Taber 2005:92).

Another insight was that mission was best accomplished as "carried out by a single, holy catholic, and apostolic church when it manages to transcend its divisions, even momentarily" (Taber 2005:93). This renewed focus on unity in the church and in mission led the Tabers away from the Brethren Church and into the fold of the Stone-Campbell Movement. Taber became very intentional concerning his convictions on the priority of the unity of the church in mission, sometimes digressing into discussions on the topic when presenting papers or writing journal articles. One example can be found when he was asked by *Missiology* to be the "evangelical" respondent to a presentation in which there was to be a Catholic respondent, a conciliar respondent, and an evangelical. Taber utilized much of his piece commenting on being called an evangelical:

> Beyond whatever doctrinal consensus there may be between persons who call themselves evangelicals, the term is commonly used in a specifically partisan and exclusive sense. Too many evangelicals, perhaps because they lack an institutional embodiment, seem obsessed with building fences between themselves and other Christians and spelling out the importance of those fences. My roots are in the evangelical movement, and in many ways my personal doctrinal position agrees with the central tenets of the evangelical consensus. But I reject the partisan and divisive use of the term and disassociate myself explicitly from all fence-building efforts in the name of evangelicalism. I serve notice that I will no longer respond to the evangelical label — not because I reject the content of evangelical faith, but because I want to maintain unbroken fellowship with all Christians, including those with whom I disagree heartily. As a matter of deep conviction, I ask to be called "Christian" without divisive qualifier. (Taber 1981:88)

I include this extended quote to provide a sense of the conviction Taber felt concerning this issue. If God's mission is carried out at its best when Christians transcend divisions, as Taber had experienced on the field, then he would no longer be partisan as a missiologist.

Finally, through autobiographical reflection, Taber "learned that sin and salvation are not purely individual matters, as the standard evangelical model seems to suggest." For Taber, it was not merely individuals, but "the structures and systems" that rebelled against God. In this light, salvation is seen as God's sovereign project "to restore all things to God's rule" (Taber 2005:93). This was often presented in his writing by a focus on the gospel of the kingdom of God (Taber 2000:134).

In seeking to understand Taber's educational approach, it is important to note that while he spent the last 34 years of his life as a missiologist, he began his career with doubts as to the validity of missiology as a separate field of study that stands on its own in the academy, or even in a graduate seminary. In his 1979 inaugural lecture as Professor of World Mission of Emmanuel School of Religion, Taber most clearly presented his philosophy on missiology and theology in seminary education. His lecture asked the question, should missiology be a separate subject in the curriculum? His answer was no, mission should not be relegated to any one department, such as Christian Doctrine or Practical Ministries. In a fragmented world that does not recognize the inherent call of mission for everyone, the situation in the seminary is lacking:

> Mission courses often have a "tacked-on" look in relation to the rest of the curriculum. One finds for instance, a course in "the biblical basis for mission," taught by a missions professor and with no apparent connection to the regular program of biblical studies. The same obtains for "theology of mission," "history of missions," and others. The situation looks precisely as though the curriculum had been designed with no thought for mission; then, as an afterthought, as a kind of remedial program or prosthesis to correct omissions in the "regular" program, missions courses were added. (Taber 2007:4)

Instead of perpetuating this afterthought, Taber insisted that mission should concern the entire faculty and students and be an integral part of every course at a seminary. Likewise, mission cannot be separated from theology. "The activity of God, the person and work of Jesus, the role of the Holy Spirit, the church, salvation, eschatology," all of these must include the "missionary motif in a central place" (Taber 2007:7).

As a trained linguist who also studied and utilized both sociology and anthropology in his missiological research and in the classroom, Taber was a proponent of the use of the social sciences for mission. Engaged in the field of translation theory and the concept of "dynamic equivalence" throughout his career (Taber and Nida 2003), Taber often pushed his students to consider the ways that the Gospel might be interpreted and understood differently in various cultural contexts. This focus on translation theory led Taber to encourage both indigenous theologizing and missionary acceptance of local interpretations of Scripture (Taber 1978; 1993). He also viewed the social sciences as "potentially useful instruments to improve [missiology's] understanding and performance," but warned that they should be used both "responsibly and critically" (Taber 2000:138).

A Comparison of the Models

Taber's educational model for missiology can be seen as very different from that of McGavran. Although similar in the incorporation of the social sciences into missiology, Taber held to a holistic vision of mission as part of the entire seminary curriculum. McGavran's vision for missiological research led to a separate institution in the Seminary that trained interdisciplinary mission specialists.

In these brief sketches we see two models of mission education from leaders of missiology from within the Stone-Campbell movement. Key features of each model includes:

McGavran Model

- Focus on researching and evaluating numerical church growth

- A focus on duplication of efforts and models that work

- The study of missiology as a separate discipline in separate programs and maybe separate schools (but accessible to all levels of church leaders)

- Missiology faculty should be specialists who work apart from Biblical Studies and Theology faculty

- Focus on understanding where resources are best utilized

- Missionary best prepares with interdisciplinary missiological education

- Establish new schools and new mission degree programs at the graduate and postgraduate levels

- Collaboration with evangelicals in mission is prioritized over ecumenical engagement

Taber Model

- Focus on aligning ourselves with the Kingdom of God and joining in the *missio Dei*

- Dynamic Translation of the Gospel

- Missiology should be evident in the entire seminary curriculum because missiology is the mother of theology

- The study of missiology within all the seminary disciplines

- Professor of Mission should work in concert with Biblical Studies and Theology faculty

- Focus on understanding culture and contextual translatability

- Missionary best prepared with biblical studies, theology, and social sciences together

- No need for new schools or even mission degree programs at the graduate or postgraduate levels

- Ecumenical collaboration with all Christians in mission is prioritized over sectarian divisions

These two models are not exhaustive and they also are in danger of reifying models that were never meant to be models. Yet these two models do provide some key differences in approaches not only to missiology, but also in the education of missionaries. These two models are both influential in missiological education in the Christian Churches/Churches of Christ institutions surveyed. While the McGavran model seems to have had the most influence on current mission and intercultural studies programs, continued value might also be found in the Taber model. I will return to this issue after a summary of findings in the survey of missions and intercultural studies degree programs.

A Brief Survey of Christian Church/ Church of Christ Missions and ICS Programs

What sort of training best prepares a cross-cultural missionary? This is the question I've been concerned with since being invited to serve as the sole Intercultural Studies faculty at Hope International University in 2012. Not only was I asked to teach everything from cultural anthropology to language acquisition to world religions, but because I had recently finished my doctoral studies, I was asked to make revisions to the ICS degree program as I saw fit, a program that had changed only slightly from its original form in 1978. Changes that were made since 1978 seemed to imitate the ICS curriculum at the graduate level at Fuller Seminary, which was understandable, as the previous professors of mission before me had received their ICS degrees at Fuller in the 1980s and 1990s.

Tasked with making these curriculum changes, my own inclination was to use the coursework at Asbury Theological Seminary's ICS programs from recent years. Additionally, I began to survey the independent Christian church/churches of Christ institutions that had missions, cross-cultural ministry or intercultural studies programs listed among their majors. Twenty institutions were identified with missions/intercultural studies programs that traditionally identify with the independent Christian Churches/Churches of Christ.

The requirements, curriculum, and faculty for seven types of degree programs (3 undergraduate programs and 4 graduate programs) were examined from the following institutions:

1. Boise Bible College

2. Central Christian College of the Bible

3. Cincinnati Bible Seminary

4. Cincinnati Christian University

5. Dallas Christian College

6. Emmanuel Christian Seminary

7. Great Lakes Christian College

8. Hope International University

9. Johnson University

10. Kentucky Christian University

11. Lincoln Christian Seminary

12. Lincoln Christian University

13. Louisville Bible College

14. Manhattan Christian College

15. Mid Atlantic Christian University

16. Milligan College

17. Nebraska Christian College

18. Ozark Christian College

19. Point University

20. St. Louis Christian College

Accreditation of Mission/ICS degree programs:

- 13 out of 20 have regional accreditation

- Seven are ABHE accredited only

- All four MDiv programs are regionally and ABHE accredited. Three out of four MDiv programs are ATS accredited. The one MDiv program that is completely online is not yet ATS accredited.

For many of the smaller institutions that began in the early to mid-20th century with the explicit goal of ministerial training for churches, accreditation was not initially an issue. This is especially true for institutions that have served the congregationally - oriented independent Christian Churches/Churches of Christ that rarely require an MDiv for ministerial ordination or consideration as a candidate for paid ministry positions. Over time, for the institutions that have grown from Bible colleges, to liberal arts colleges, to universities with multiple colleges, accreditation has been an important element in continuing to attract new students and ensure a level of quality and academic rigor.

Three institutions have had MDiv programs since their inception as an institution: Cincinnati Bible Seminary, Emmanuel Christian Seminary, and Lincoln Christian Seminary. These three MDiv programs are accredited by the Association of Theological Schools. A fourth institution, Hope International University, has recently added a regionally accredited, completely online MDiv program, building on its 20 years of experience with online programs and recognizing the need for continuing education of ministers in fulltime positions. ATS does not at this time accredit online MDiv programs in which more than 2/3 of the coursework is online.

Both Taber and McGavran worked for institutions that maintained regional accreditation and sought the highest qualified faculty available to fill open positions as their colleagues. Taber encouraged all students considering long - term cross - cultural ministry to complete the MDiv degree in which 15 of the 90 semester hours could be focused on missiology. McGavran not only encouraged pre-field training through study at the School of World Mission, but worked for Fuller to become the institution of choice for furloughing and mid-career missionaries to continue their missiological education and research.

Faculty in Mission/ICS Degree Programs:

Full-time Mission/ICS faculty: 25

Holding a terminal missiology/ICS degree (either DMiss or PhD ICS): 8

Highest degree and awarding institution:

DMiss, Asbury Theological Seminary

PhD, ICS, Asbury Theological Seminary

DMiss, Biola

MA, Columbia Seminary

MDiv, Emmanuel Christian Seminary

DMin, Emmanuel Christian Seminary

MA, Fuller Theological Seminary

PhD, ICS, Fuller Theological Seminary (2)

PhD, Linguistics, Indiana University

MA, Johnson University

MA, Lincoln Christian Seminary (2)

MDiv, Lincoln Christian Seminary (3)

PhD, ICS, Southern Baptist Theological Seminary

DMin, Trinity Evangelical Divinity School

PhD, ICS, Trinity Evangelical Divinity School

MMin, Trinity Theological Seminary

PhD, New Testament, Union Theological Seminary

MA, Sociology, University of Cincinnati

MS, Foreign Languages, University of Tennessee

MA, Linguistics, University of Texas

DMin, Westminster Theological Seminary

With as many fulltime missions/ICS faculty, it is surprising that only eight hold terminal degrees in missions and ICS. In institutions following a McGavran model of specialization and separate programs for ICS, it would seem that as faculty retire in these programs, more candidates holding the PhD in Intercultural Studies will be considered and hired. It is surprising, yet reassuring to find 16 out of the 25 faculty holding degrees from institutions outside of the Stone-Campbell church movement.

It is consistent with a Taber model to find that in the two institutions in which he had the most influence, Milligan College and Emmanuel Christian Seminary, the missions professors hold a PhD in Linguistics and a PhD in New Testament. Both have served as Bible translators and translation consultants, as Taber had before serving as faculty.

Names of Specific Degree Programs:

BA/BS in Christian Ministry (Bible/ministry) with a concentration or major or minor in Missions/ICS:

1. Boise Bible College

2. Central Christian College of the Bible

3. Cincinnati Christian University

4. Dallas Christian College

5. Great Lakes Christian College

6. Kentucky Christian University

7. Louisville Bible College

8. Manhattan Christian College

9. Milligan College (the Missions major concentration is a Bible/Ministry major with 6 units of Mission courses and 18 units of a sociology minor)

10. Ozark Chistian College

11. Point Univeristy

BA in Intercultural Studies (multiple concentrations):

1. Hope International University

2. Johnson University

3. Lincoln Christian University

BA/BS in Cross-Cultural Ministry:

1. Mid Atlantic Christian University

BA in World Missions:

1. Nebraska Christian College

BA/BS in Intercultural and Urban Missions:

1. St. Louis Christian College

BA in Cross-Cultural Business Administration:

1. Hope International University

BA/BS in Cross-Cultural Media Communications:

1. Johnson University

BA/BS in Global Community Health:

1. Johnson University

MA in Intercultural Studies:

1. Johnson University (ONLINE)

2. Lincoln Christian University

MA in Ministry with ICS specialization/concentration:

1. Hope International University (ONLINE)

2. Lincoln Christian University (ONLINE)

MAR Leadership Studies: Urban and Intercultural Ministry:

1. Cincinnati Bible Seminary

MDiv with concentration/specialization in Christian World Mission/Intercultural Studies:

1. Cincinnati Bible Seminary

2. Emmanuel Christian Seminary

3. Hope International University (ONLINE)

4. Lincoln Christian Seminary (HYBRID: up to 2/3 online)

Nomenclature in these programs displays a shifting that has progressed in many institutions from "missions" to "cross-cultural ministry" to "intercultural studies." Some institutions, including where I teach, previously even used the term "church growth" in their ministry and missions degrees.

Tracking Fuller's School of World Missions (and Institute of Church Growth), we find that while Fuller was among the first to transition to degrees in intercultural studies, the name of the school itself did not incorporate the term until much later than some other institutions. A timeline of some of some of the nomenclature changes is provided by Charles Kraft (Kraft 2005:237-239). I have added key dates for Asbury Theological Seminary and Biola for comparison.

1965: McGavran and Tippet are the founding dean and faculty of the School of World Missions and Institute of Church Growth.

1975: Fuller launches a cross-cultural studies program.

1976: Fuller begins to offer a PhD in Missiology.

1981:   Fuller begins to offer a PhD in Intercultural Studies

1983:   Biola launches the Cook School of Intercultural Studies, offering the PhD in ICS

1983:   Asbury Theological Seminary began the E. Stanley Jones School of World Mission and Evangelism offering the PhD in ICS

1991:   Fuller offers a new curriculum, containing 15 concentrations in Missiology.

2003:   The Fuller School of World Mission is renamed the School of Intercultural Studies.

My own current institution, Hope International University, in the shadow of both Fuller and Biola, closely followed Fuller Seminary's pattern. Cross-Cultural Missions was a concentration in a BA in Ministry and Church Growth, until a major revision beginning in the fall of 1994 dropped the use of the term Church Growth and a BA in Intercultural Studies began. Further highlighting the influence of McGavran on HIUs programs, when Pacific Christian College reorganized as five colleges and changed its name to Hope International University in 1997, *Donald A. McGavran University* was a serious name being suggested by the president and the Board of Trustees.

Other recent nomenclature changes in missions and ICS programs are notable and may be pointing to a further continuing trend. In the fall of 2015, Moody Bible Institute will officially change the name of its "mission" program to "Intercultural Studies." Multnomah University announced in March 2015 that they are changing their "Intercultural Studies" nomenclature to "Global Studies." These two name changes are significant through the lenses of McGavran and Taber models.

On the one hand, the largest Bible colleges in the nation are now following in the McGavran model of specialized programs in intercultural studies. While in many institutions this change is touted as necessary to reflect the varied opportunities available to graduates with a degree in "intercultural studies," as opposed to a degree in the more colonially termed "mission," it still points to a very specialized evangelical Christian view of educational preparation for those called to minister interculturally. On the other hand, the shift to "global studies," "area studies," or even "international relations," not only recognizes that there are already fields of study within the academy at the undergraduate level that provide the social scientific perspective needed for intercultural ministry, but also that these fields truly provide a degree that is multi-faceted and not specifically identified as Christian. This would be a more thoroughly Taber model at the undergraduate level. Even in the undergraduate institution where Taber last taught more than 30 years ago, Milligan College, a ministry student with a desire to concentrate in Christian Missions completes the Bible/Ministry major, two 3 unit missions courses (Introduction to Christian Mission and History of Christian Mission), and a 18 unit minor in Sociology. It is expected that the student will then attend seminary to further prepare for ministry.

One final category from the research will be examined to reveal more of McGavran and Taber models in our undergraduate and graduate institutions.

Number of semester units/hours required for program completion:

- Most undergraduate missions/ICS programs are 120-130 semester hours/units

- Exceptions: Three are over 130 hours because of large Bible coursework requirements: Central Christian College of the Bible: 138 hours (54 hours of Bible); Louisville Bible College: 140 hours (51 hours of Bible); Mid Atlantic Christian University: 137 hours (50 hours

  of Bible)

- Most undergraduate missions/ICS concentrations require significant biblical studies semester units/hours:

  - About 30 units of Biblical Studies required

  - 4 programs are 45 units or higher

  - 2 programs are under 25 units of biblical studies:

  - One is 21, the other is 12 units, which is the lowest requirement.

- Undergraduate missions/ICS specific major coursework unit/hour requirements:

  - Undergraduate: 9, 12 (2), 16, 17 (2), 18 (3) 21, 22, 24, 30, 33 (2) 36 (2), 37, 39

  - Graduate: 15 (3), 12, 36

While graduate programs incorporating intercultural studies are fairly standardized, with MDiv concentrations maxing at 12-15 units and most MA ICS programs at 36 units, undergraduate programs vary significantly in category, both in the number of biblical studies requirements and in the number of ICS/missions specific course requirements. Again, this points to programs and institutions that are following different models. In general, larger numbers of units in biblical studies seem to be a carryover of the particular identities of institutions that began as Bible colleges. Lower numbers of biblical studies requirements are found in both institutions that have either never identified as Bible colleges or have transitioned their missions/ICS programs into separate tracks and schools from ministry and biblical studies degrees. Through my McGavran and Taber model lenses, the higher the number of required ICS specific courses in an undergraduate program, the more the program fits into the McGavran model of missiological education.

Conclusions? Pulled in Two Directions

The more I look over the survey of the mission/ICS programs in these 20 institutions through the lenses of the McGavran and Taber models, the more I am pulled in two directions. In some ways, these models represent deep institutional identities, convictions, and priorities. While one could critique the McGavran model of missiological education as increasingly disconnected from biblical scholarship and theology or of providing a limited Christian application of the social sciences, this represents a particularly evangelical conviction for engaging in effective mission in all contexts of the world. Likewise, the Taber model of missiological education can be critiqued as being susceptible to a view of mission that is overly inclusive of all activity as mission and allows the social sciences to overly influence theological vision, yet this represents a more universally Christian perspective of our participation in the growth of the Kingdom of God, sometimes in unquantifiable ways.

In the Stone-Campbell movement, we see a stronger emphasis on mission majors and degree programs in those institutions that began as small Bible colleges in the 20th century. The older institutions that began in the 19th century are more focused on commonly found social science majors for those interested in cross-cultural ministry or mission training. These majors include sociology, religious studies, and global studies. Again, these appear to be related to particular institutional identities.

This reveals a pattern of institutions that began as Bible colleges to have included some sort of concentration/emphasis or degree in missions early on in the institution's history. Many of these institutions began in the early 1900's and were started in reaction to what was viewed as liberalism in biblical interpretation and biblical criticism in the more well-established American universities and seminaries.

The Christian Churches/Churches of Christ institutions followed in this pattern. As the Stone-Campbell unity movement began to divide in the early 20th century, the more formalized churches identified with the structured denomination: Christian Church (Disciples of Christ). These churches continued to rely on the older Stone-Campbell training institutions: Brite Divinity School at Texas Christian University, Butler School of Religion (now Christian Theological Seminary) in Indianapolis, Lexington Theological Seminary, KY, and at the Disciples Divinity Houses in the Divinity Schools of University of Chicago, Vanderbilt, and Yale.

In the Christian Church (Disciples of Christ) affiliated colleges and universities, all started in the 19th century or modeled after the older institutions, not a single institution has a missions/intercultural studies major at the undergraduate level, yet most have international studies or global studies, neither of which has an expressed intent for preparing graduates for intercultural Christian ministry. The vast majority do not have a Bible/Ministry major. Those who are interested in pursuing a seminary degree in preparation for ministry are best suited by an undergraduate degree in religion. Indeed, ministerial ordination in this now mainline denominational church requires an MDiv. Yet, the very inclusive view of mission in the Christian Churches (Disciples of Christ) is not one that many in the Christian Churches/Churches of Christ find consistent with a more evangelistic vision.

Certainly there are answers beyond a 'mission is evangelism,' 'mission is everything' debate. How can we move forward? We need to look closely at each other's programs and begin a process of identifying what our priorities are. What's missing? What is there that is no longer relevant? Should we be creating more schools of World Mission, or should we seek to add mission into more of our other programs? Or, is there a way to accomplish both?

One missing piece of the puzzle is a long term look at the outcomes of the programs surveyed. What are graduates actually doing with their degrees? How many are serving in traditional cross-cultural ministry contexts? How many are doing something else? Are significant numbers of graduates of undergraduate intercultural studies programs using their education in fields other than church supported ministries?

Unlike many academic disciplines, there is not a standard model for academic programs in missiology and intercultural studies. It would seem that part of the ongoing calling and mission of an organization called the Association of Professors of Mission would be to continue to research, study and compare more of our institutions and programs. Would it not be beneficial for our organization to even provide guidance, resources and suggestions in this area? Could a basic standard curriculum be suggested for the undergraduate level? Or, would the suggestion be that an undergraduate level of study in missions/intercultural studies must not be proliferated or encouraged, but that emerging Bible colleges and small Christian universities should add sociology, anthropology or global studies departments to serve the needs of those students preparing to serve interculturally? These are questions for a broader discussion, a discussion that I hope the contribution of this paper will ignite by providing us with two missiological models that will help us sharpen the focus of our missiological educational priorities.

Works Cited:

Blowers, Paul
    2004   "Barclay, James Turner (1807-1874)." In *The Encylopedia of the Stone-Campbell Movement*, 69–70. Grand Rapids, MI: W.B. Eerdmans Pub.

Bosch, David Jacobus
    1991   *Transforming Mission: Paradigm Shifts in Theology of Mission.* American Society of Missiology Series 16. Maryknoll, NY: Orbis Books.

Chapman, Robert S.
    2010   "Christian Missionary Fellowship's Thirty Years in Turkana." Unpublished Manuscript.

Elliston, Edgar J., Robert S. Chapman, Randall Nelson, Edie Nelson, and Donna Elliston
    1979 "CMF-Daystar Turkana Survey Report." CMF Archives.

Hunter, George G.
    1992   "The Legacy of Donald A. McGavran." *International Bulletin of Missionary Research* 16 (4): 158–62.

Kraft, Charles H.
    2005   *SWM/SIS at Forty: A Participant/Observer's View of Our History.* Pasadena, CA: William Carey Library.

Lines, Kevin P.
    1998   "The Continued Importance of a Mission Moratorium." M.A.R. Thesis, Johnson City, TN: Emmanuel School of Religion.

McGavran, Donald A.
    1986   "My Pilgrimmage in Mission." *International Bulletin of Missionary Research* 10 (2): 53–58.

Nida, Eugene Albert, and Charles R. Taber
2003 *The Theory and Practice of Translation*. Boston, MA: Brill.

Skreslet, Stanley H.
2012 *Comprehending Mission: The Questions Methods, Themes, Problems, and Prospects of Mission*. American Society of Missiology Series. Maryknoll, Y: Orbis Books.

Taber, Charles R.
1973 "Unevangelized Peoples: Whose Responsibility?" *Milligan College Missiological Quarterly* 1 (2): 3.

1978 "Limits of Indigenization in Theology." *Missiology* 6 (1): 53–79.

1981 "Some Evangelical Questions." *Missiology* 9 (1): 87–91.

1986 "Book Review: Momentous Decisions in Missions Today, by Donald A. McGavran." *International Bulletin of Missionary Research* 10 (3): 139.

1993 "Is There More Than One Way to Do Theology: Anthropological Comments on the Doing of Theology." *Didaskalia (Otterburne, Man.)* 5 (1): 3–18.

2000 *To Understand the World, to Save the World: The Interface Between Missiology and the Social Sciences*. Christian Mission and Modern Culture; Harrisburg, PA: Trinity Press International.

2005 "My Pilgrimage in Mission." *International Bulletin of Missionary Research* 29 (2): 89–93.

n.d. *Graduate Education for World Mission*. Emmanuel Reflection Series 23. Johnson City, TN: Emmanuel School of Religion.

Appendix A: Missions and Intercultural Studies Programs in 20 Independent Christian Church/Churches of Christ Institutions:

1. BA/BS in Christian Ministry (Bible/ministry) with a concentration or major or minor in ICS:

Institution	Accreditation	Total Units	Bib Studies	ICS units	Internship?
Boise Bible College	ABHE	128	45	16	2-4 units STM and 8-12 weeks
Central Christian College of the Bible	ABHE	138	54	22	3 units= 300 hours
Cincinnati Christian University	Regional, ABHE	120	33	18	9 units= 7 months or 3 months + practicum class
Dallas Christian College	ABHE	129	21	12	3 units
Great Lakes Christian College	Regional, ABHE	130 (BS only)	44	37	3 unit= 12 weeks

Kentucky Christian University	Regional	121	63 (includes ministry units)	9	12 units = 6-8 months
Louisville Bible College	ABHE	140	51	21	2 units of missions internship
Manhattan Christian College	Regional, ABHE	125	30	12 (emphasis), 6 (track)	
Milligan College	Regional	128	12	24 (6+18 unit Sociology minor)	2-4 units= 2 month internship
Ozark Christian College	ABHE	128	57	30	4 units
Point University	Regional	124	39	17	Flexible

2. BA in Intercultural Studies:

Institution	Accreditation	Total Units	Bib Studies	ICS units	Internship?
Hope International University	Regional, ABHE	120	30	33	1 unit= 8-12 months + 6 units of practicum classes
Johnson University	Regional, ABHE	120	33	18-30 (depends on concentration)	3 units= summer internship

| Lincoln Christian University | Regional, ABHE | 130 | 30 | 39 | | 12 units= Semester long, 4 units= 2 months |

BA/BS in Cross-Cultural Ministry:

Institution	Accreditation	Total Units	Bib Studies	ICS units	Internship?
Mid Atlantic Christian University	Regional	137	50	36	6 credits, flexible

BA in World Missions:

Institution	Accreditation	Total Units	Bib Studies	ICS units	Internship?
Nebraska Christian College	ABHE	138	38	24	12 units= 1 semester outside the US

3. Other Specialized BA Programs:

BA/BS in Intercultural and Urban Missions:

Institution	Accreditation	Total Units	Bib Studies	ICS units	Internship?
St. Louis Christian College	ABHE	127	42	18	3 units. Flexible.

BA in Cross-Cultural Business Administration:

Institution   Accreditation Total Units Bib Studies ICS units   Internship?

Hope International University	Regional	122	18	ICS: 12-21 Bus/Mgt: 36-45	3 units

BA/BS in Cross-Cultural Media Communications:

Institution   Accreditation   Total Units   Bib Studies ICS units   Internship?

Johnson University	Regional, ABHE	122	30	ICS: 18 Media Comm: 21	3 units

BA/BS in Global Community Health:

Institution   Accreditation Total Units Bib Studies ICS units Internship?

Johnson University	Regional	129	30	ICS: 18 Public Health: 29	3 units

4. MA in Intercultural Studies:

Institution   Accreditation   Total Units   Internship?

Johnson University (ONLINE)	Regional, ABHE	36-48 (depends on concentration)	3 unit integrative project
Lincoln Christian University	Regional, ABHE	36	

5. MA in Ministry with ICS specialization/concentration:

Institution	Accreditation	Total Units	Bib Studies	ICS units	Internship?
Hope International University (ONLINE)	Regional, ABHE	42	18	12	Final Project
Lincoln Christian University (ONLINE)	Regional, ABHE, ATS	36	6	9	3 units

6. MAR Leadership Studies: Urban and Intercultural Ministry:

Institution	Accreditation	Total Units	ICS units
Cincinnati Bible Seminary	ATS	54	15

7. MDiv with concentration/specialization in Christian World Mission/Intercultural Studies:

Institution	Accreditation	Total Units	ICS units
Cincinnati Bible Seminary	Regional, ATS	90	15
Emmanuel Christian Seminary	Regional, ATS	90	15
Hope International University (ONLINE)	Regional, ABHE	72	12
Lincoln Christian Seminary (HYBRID: up to 2/3 online)	Regional, ABHE, ATS	75	15

APPENDIX B: Abnormal and Common Courses in Undergraduate ICS and Missions Degree Programs.

Abnormal undergraduate courses (courses occurring three times or less in the programs curriculum lists)

- Language Acquistion (1)
- World Geography (1)
- Church in Context / Contextualization (2)
- Missiology (1)
- Evangelism (1)
- Church Growth (0)
- Sprititual Conflict / Spritual Warfare (2)
- Intro to Islam (1) / History of Islam (1)
- Cross-Cultural Counseling (1)
- Cross-Cultural Psychology (1)

- Latin American Cultures (1)
- Business as Mission (1)
- Linguistics (1)
- TESOL (3)
- Race and Ethnicity (2)
- Sociology of Religion (1)
- Sociology of Family (1)
- Dynamics of Culture Change (1)
- Community Development (2)
- Mission Administration (1)
- Short - Term Mission Trip Leadership

Common Undergraduate Courses (courses occurring in more than 5 programs):

- Foundations or Introduction to Missions, Christian World Mission

- Cultural Anthropology/Cultural Anthropology for Ministry/Applied Anthropology

- Living and Working Cross-Culturally, Strategies for Mission

- Intercultural Communication

- Urban Ministry

- World Religions/Comparative Religions

- Research Methods

- Contemporary Mission Methods

- Biblical Theology of Mission

- History of Mission

- World Christian Movements (Perspectives course outline)

Theology as Christian Self - Description and Academic Inquiry:

Thinking with Hans Frei on Mission Studies

DANIEL D. SHIN

DOI: 10.7252/Paper. 000053

About the Author
Daniel D. Shin is currently Bishop Cornelius and Dorothey Henderson/E. Stanley Jones Chair of Evangelism at Gammon/ITC in Atlanta, Ga. He teaches in the areas of evangelism, mission, and theology.

Introduction

The aim of this essay is to reflect on the 2015 APM Conference theme "What's In a Name? Assessing Mission Studies Program Titles" in conversation with Hans W. Frei.[1] In the essay, I focus on Frei's *Types of Christian Theology* to explore his understanding of theology as both Christian self-description and academic inquiry, which was informed substantially by his analysis of Friedrich Schleiermacher's proposal to include theology as a professional school at the University of Berlin. It is fitting that Frei's historical/methodological reflection on the case of Berlin is undertaken in examining metamorphoses of mission studies titles and programs as both cases involve making of the new at the programmatic level of educational institutions. The essay begins with a brief discussion of Paul Ricoeur's notion of tradition as interplay between sedimentation and innovation to show that, as it was true in the case of Schleiermacher's correlation of *Wissenschaft* and *Glaube*, changes in mission studies programs and titles involve poetic imagination, especially the notion of experiment (Ricoeur 1984:52-87). Then, this analysis proceeds to, first of all, Schleiermacher's appeal to the theme of professionalization in his efforts to come to terms with the practical nature of theology related to the context of the church and other social ends. Secondly, intricately related to professionalization, it attends to Schleiermacher's handling of the problematic of irreducible

---

1   Hans W. Frei's contribution in theological hermeneutics, Christology and theological ethics, and theological method has been recognized widely as one of the key impetus in the development of postliberal theology, and its significance for practical theology, in particular, missiology is yet to be fully explored. His major published works are the following: Hans W. Frei, *The Eclipse of Biblical Narrative: A Study in the Eighteenth and Nineteenth Century Hermeneutics* (New Haven: Yale University Press, 1974); idem, *The Identity of Jesus Christ* (Eugene, Ore.: Wipf and Stock Publishers, 1997); idem, *Theology and Narrative: Selected Essays*, ed. George Hunsinger and William Placher (New York: Oxford University Press, 1993); idem, *Types of Christian Theology*, ed. George Hunsinger and William C. Placher (New Haven: Yale University Press, 1992); hereafter cited as *Types*.

Christian specificity of theology in the public of the academy by way of an embryonic understanding of the social sciences.[2] And lastly, I will conclude with some reflections on the implications that arise from this investigation.

A. Nomenclature and Poetic Imagination

In recent years, some Christian institutions of higher learning have relinquished the birthright of traditional nomenclature of their mission studies programs and adopted names such as Intercultural Studies or World Christianity, and some have offered dual degrees in theology and other disciplines, such as social work. The changes in nomenclature and program are complex phenomena with deep implications, so we raise the question "What's in a name?" To situate the phenomenon in the larger context of the Christian tradition, it is helpful to consider what Paul Ricoeur says about tradition as interplay between sedimentation and innovation. Sedimentation results from the paradigms that constitute the typology of emplotment, which were originally born from the labor of the productive imagination itself, but through layers of history they culminate in existing forms (Ricoeur 1984: 65-70). Innovation is correlative to sedimentation but functions as its counterpoint. Whereas the paradigmatic order in prefigured world of action is governed by rules leading to sedimentation, innovation is not servile to rules, though it is rule governed than being born from nothing, and makes calculated deviations. Its rule governed deformation deviates to contest sedimentation in order to create something new in configuration and refiguration. Understood within the larger context of the story of Christianity, nominal changes can be an ecstatic moment of *poiesis* that entails both hermeneutics of suspicion and restoration at all levels, including its title, curriculum, faculty hire, and student recruitment, even to the point of the death of the old and the birth of the new.

Nomenclature and program changes are ruled inscribed calculated deviations that suggest something about the present conditions, the actors, and the institutions involved that actualize the story of Christianity through

---

2   For further discussion on the three publics, the church, the society, and the academy, see David Tracy, *The Analogical Imagination* (New York: The Crossroad Publishing Company, 1981), 3-31.

productive judgment, manifesting interplay between sedimentation and innovation. It is poetic imagination at work in performative mimesis that is not a passive response to the experience of reality but a creative transfiguration of the field of action to achieve meaning and being in history (Ricoeur 1992: 52-55 and 143-148). Administrators, faculty, students, and constituent religious and social institutions, analogous to the readers of a story, are not mechanistically fated and scripted to submissively follow a narrow plot, but critically and constructively enact the tradition, grasp its meaning, experience and express pleasure and/or displeasure, complete the holes and lacunae of indetermination in history (Ricoeur 1984: 77). And as Ricoeur suggests, this interplay between sedimentation and innovation involves creative capacity for proliferation of divergences, especially in art as ethical laboratory of experiments, which accord narratives subversive and dangerous qualities. To be underscored here is the notion of experiment—involving risks of being subversive and dangerous—inherent in prefiguration, configuration, and refiguration shaped by various teleological judgments.

B. Theology as Christian Self-Description and Academic Inquiry

To examine in specific details the experimental character of mission studies nomenclature and programs, it is illuminating to think with Hans Frei about mission studies as either Christian self-description or academic inquiry, or both, especially as they negotiate between internal norms and affairs and external impingements. In his own experiment of interplay between sedimentation and innovation in reconceiving theology, Frei engages Schleiermacher in his essay "The Case of Berlin, 1810." Frei's choice of Schleiermacher as his interlocutor is logical not only because he finds his proposal "highly instructive" for his own construal of theology, but also because of Schleiermacher's vital role in the establishment of theology faculty at the University of Berlin, which eventually became the prototypical German university and the model for many universities in Europe and North America (Frei 1992: 95-116). As the prototypical university, Berlin led the way in promoting the ideals of *Wissenschaft*, which was usually understood as science or theory of reason involving free exercise of rational inquiry into the universal, transcendental principles that encompass all fields of inquiry and organize them into systematic, intelligible totalities. Its signature mark was free, rational inquiry and this was clearly evident in how the philosophy faculty was considered to be the most important in the university in embodying the ideals of *Wissenschaft*.

However, Frei points out that the birth of this university involved complications because the Prussian government, which had the right to regulate the temporal affairs of the church, employed theologians as members of the state bureaucracy with their right to non-interference as intellectuals but also as instructors of church professionals. It created an awkward situation in delegating the training of ministers to a university that had mixed thoughts about the compatibility of training clergy with its own *Wissenschaftlich* ideals. An intense debate ensued concerning "the public character of the understanding informing theology" in the university because of the challenge to do justice to both church training and *Glaube* as well as to *Wissenschaftlich* principles of general explanation that applied across all disciplines.[3]

Theology and Professionalization

It is within this context of heated debate on the suitability of theological training in the university that Frei explores Schleiermacher's understanding of academic theology. Schleiermacher's proposal was not the only one on the table but eventually was accepted in thinking about the citizenship of theological faculty in the university. He was certainly an academic and recognized fully the preeminent place of philosophy among the university faculties and thought that the task of the university is to teach the young to "regard everything from the point of view of *Wissenschaft*" (Frei 1992: 110). However, he was also "a full-blooded Christian theologian" who would

---

3   For instance, Fichte responded to the question of the suitability of practical theological training in the university by arguing that any school which proscribes the use of reason and asserts itself a priori as an unfathomable mystery should be excluded from the university. This meant that for theology to be included in the university it had to abandon its claim to privileged knowledge of God and practical instruction in the ministerial arts. Frei comments that there is in Fichte "no hankering after the inclusion of praxis in his notion of theory." Frei, "The Case of Berlin, 1810," 106; idem, "Types of Academic Theology," in *Types*, 118.

not accept the reduction of theology to philosophy, and made a complex argument defending the rightful place of theology in the university by appeals to the traditions of *Weltanschauung*, *Bildung*, and *Kenntnisse*.

All three traditions were important but he made a special appeal to the time-honored tradition of *Kenntnisse* through which he envisioned a union of *Wissenschaftlich* theological inquiry with the professional, practical training of ministers in the church.[4] Schleiermacher argued for the importance of theology by advocating the legitimate inclusion of professional schools, i.e., theology, medicine, and law, in the university curriculum (Frei 1992: 118, 126-127, and 132). He thought that instructions in professional schools stimulate students to make an intimate connection between theory and praxis in order that they may acquire both practical and conceptual skills that are necessary to master a field. The aim of such professional schools is not necessarily *Wissenschaft* but one of founding the socially indispensable practices through theory in the tradition of *Kenntnisse*, which is defined as "something like the 'abilities' or 'cognitive skills' requisite for carrying out the given practical work" (Frei 1993: 191). Schleiermacher argued that "Christian theology is … the compass of those skills [*Kenntnisse*, once again] and practical rules [*Kunstregeln*, rules that are the fruit of practical skill rather than theoretical deduction] without whose possession and use a cohesive direction of the Christian church, i.e., a church government, is not possible" (Frei 1992: 113). On that account, Schleiermacher argued that professional schools do not bear an intrinsic relation to *Wissenschaft*, but because of the pragmatic, socially indispensable nature of their disciplines in the public domain, university citizenship should be granted.

---

4   Frei, "The Case of Berlin, 1810," 107. The very structure of the German University reflected its commitment to the *Wissenschaftlich* studies as well as professional training. Unlike the British and French education systems, the German University is an institution between the Academy of Sciences that specializes in pure research and the professional school that concerns itself with instruction of special skills. This meant that in the end the University of Berlin was unable to thoroughly embody the ideal of *Wissenschaft* and resulted in an orderly eclecticism. But Schleiermacher's response to those who criticized this eclecticism was, "See if you can come up with anything better before you scrap this proposal." Frei, "Theology in the University," in *Types*, 111-112.

In this analysis, Frei underscores that Schleiermacher argued for the citizenship of theology in the university on the status of the ministry as one of the professions in the modern sense (Frei 1992: 112-115). His professional understanding of theology was reflective of the legal-institutional and cultural milieu of Germany during that period which viewed theologians as professionals whose expertise was deemed important by the governmental authority for the interest of the public domain. Theologians were not considered as divines but "simply professionals, just as we have intellectuals, novelists, licensed beauticians, and therapists today. There is a whole culture of professionalism, and in regard to theology, Berlin led the way" (Frei 1992: 115). Thus, Schleiermacher's argument for the place of theology in the university is not made on systematic philosophical grounds but on legal-institutional and cultural grounds.

Theology and Christian Self-Description

Correlative to the theme of professionalization of theology is its irreducible Christian specificity (Frei 1992: 118-119). In his essay "Barth and Schleiermacher: Divergence and Convergence," Frei recalls Schleiermacher's position that the three professional schools have "their original *raison d'être* prior to or outside the university" and that they are special schools that the state has established with distinct privileges because of the essential needs they serve in the public domain. Frei writes, "Theology is a practical discipline as a whole and not merely a theoretical or scientific enterprise—either of a transcendental or of an empirical character—with an, as it were, external aim" (Frei 1993: 190-192). Professionalization of theology, more specifically, training of parsons for ministry, with a theoretical foundation in *Kenntnisse* is inextricably linked to external social and practical aims related to the church as a cultural-religious tradition and community. We see here a socio-linguistic turn to the church focused on impartation and acquisition of irreducibly Christian cultural-religious tradition at the primary level of participatory and internal access to a mode of faith, a cultural-religious tradition, and at the secondary level of descriptive and critical appraisals of its norms, conventions, and internal logic.

Frei goes on to note that Schleiermacher's understanding of theory in professional faculties of theology, law, and medicine was not about the high-powered explanation of the conditions for the possibility of the practice, but "more like the grammatical remarks that further us in the use and informal reflection on the rules of the use of a language we are learning, to appropriate the language of the later Wittgenstein and his little flock" (Frei 1992: 112). Theology is viewed as a positive enterprise that does not inherently cohere as an intrinsic part of a universal philosophical foundation, e.g., transcendental philosophy, but involves "the acquisition and impartation of the continuing tradition of a community—an ecclesiastical culture, if you will—by means of the proper use of its language under conditions of cultic continuity and social change" (Frei 1992: 112). This understanding of theology is informed deeply by a sense of its own history, a continuity of language and custom commonly understood as tradition.[5] Simply stated, theology is Christian self-description, though not without mediation, at least, *ad hoc* correlation.

Without denying the importance of *Wissenschaftlich* approach to theology, Schleiermacher stressed theology as part of "the heritable social currency of a specific religious community, the Christian church. Theology is a self-critical inquiry into the use of its language under a norm furnished within that pious linguistic community, especially "the constant transition from the Christian religious affections to their kerygmatic, poetic, rhetorical, and finally their descriptively didactic linguistic shape" (Frei 1993: 191). He identified "the irreducible specificity of Christianity at the primary level of a 'mode of faith,' a cultural-religious tradition, and

---

5   Theology is then for Schleiermacher not found on general principles or specific method with a universal philosophical foundation that unequivocally sets the criteria for meaning, meaningfulness, and truth of theological statements. He argued, "Any purely formal, universal canon of reason which adjudicates the coherence, consistency, and intelligibility of the 'method' governing a particular field of study cannot do so in this case," and "there cannot be a priority to theology of any specific (material) philosophical scheme.... In short, neither formally nor materially can philosophy be a foundational discipline for theology." What he is concerned about is that philosophical proofs of truth and *a priori* generalization about the meaning of Christian claims would result in a reduction of Christianity to the general ideal of humane culture. Under such a scheme, theology becomes a straightforward application of logically prior philosophical and historical theological insights to logically subsequent and practical matters of the church. Frei, "Barth and Schleiermacher," *Theology and Narrative*, 189-192.

a linguistic community," and second, "he claimed it as the second level of the language of the community in expert hands for the practical aim of organizing the skills of governance" (Frei 1992: 114). Frei writes:

> Theology … is a practical discipline; it is in effect part of learning the grammar of a linguistic symbol system; it is Christian self-description under some norm for its specific language use. No matter what it may entail logically in matters of theory, it is part of the praxis, the ruled practice of culture, part of social tradition enacted by a participant, an agent who knows how to use the language in its appropriate context. The formulations of the Christian confessions and their interpretations may be taken that way (Frei 1992: 126).

This is helpful in understanding how Schleiermacher's understanding of theology as religion specific informed the connections he made between the philosophical, historical, and dogmatic aspects of theology and the practical aim of theology oriented toward worship, preaching, instruction, and pastoral care. It was a strategic move that created space for Schleiermacher to distinguish theology from other areas of culture and their study, and granted the faculty and the students permission to develop "internal or participative access" to its historical shape, reality, and its truth-claims as a universal reality in one particular cultural form (Frei 1993: 189).

In this turn toward the practical and irreducible Christian specificity, Schleiermacher has conferred upon modern theology an understanding of theology that is affiliated with ethics or philosophy of religion in his day or commonly known today as the social sciences, especially social anthropology, which Frei sees as a natural cognate discipline to theology. Theology understood as second-level descriptive and critical appraisals of its own first-level language and actions under a norm internal to the community itself resembles social science more than philosophy (Frei 1993: 127). Frei writes,

> Theology is as intimately and basically explained by a sociology of knowledge as by a philosophy of the knowledge of reality. In fact, to the extent that Schleiermacher advocated the primacy of the partial aim of theology within the Church, the nearest discipline to it is a social science that describes, and in describing explains, the way

theological language functions as a part of the web of relations constituting the community of which it is a part (Frei 1992: 114-115).

It is important to note here that theology as Christian self-description is also academic inquiry by way of the social sciences along with other disciplines.[6]

Making a long story short, the University of Berlin was in actuality eclectic rather than embodying a single coherent *Wissenschaftlich* idea, and it embraced the task of training students for the public professions such as theology which could claim an equal right to that of *Wissenschaft* in a university along with the arts and sciences. The university produced an orderly eclecticism, combining the idea of intellectual unity and supremacy of *Wissenschaft* with the actual diversity of an institution of higher learning that included theology as a practical discipline.[7] It was not perfect but it enabled the preservation and development of the irreducible specificity

---

6   Frei is wary of general conceptual tools becoming a supertheory that overwhelms Christian specificity, so he suggests that the relation between theology and the social sciences must be kept external so that the use of a social-scientific explanation in theology can remain a flexible and open-ended thought experiment, rather than functioning as an aspect of philosophy as general explanatory theory—*Wissenschaftstheorie*—which becomes a much more basic outlook. Another chief concern in keeping the relation between theology and the social sciences external is to protect the role of intentional agency. For Frei's further discussion on the relation between intentional action and social structure, including his discussion of Peter Winch, Clifford Geertz, Marxist structuralists, and Habermas, see Frei, "Types of Academic Theology," in *Types*, 128-129.

7   Frei, "The Case of Berlin, 1810," 112. Schleiermacher's strategy was a nonreductionistic dialectical relation between descriptive and explanatory modes in the science of ethics—culture and history—which would do justice to "the nonrepeatability and individuality of phenomena and to the distinctiveness of their description from the agent's or experiencer's point of view, while at the same time permitting not only appeal to patterns of similarity but to lawlike causal connections between sequential human events and social structures." Frei, "Theology in the University," in *Types*, 114.

of Christian self-description and professional development in academic theology, and at the same time a correlation between theology and *Wissenschaft* under an embryonic understanding of social science.[8]

Schleiermacher's vision for the university was to achieve a dialectical resolution of theology as both *Wissenschaft* and practical, distinctive activity of the church (Frei 1992: 118). Though not without difficulty, Schleiermacher sought to maintain the tension between theory and practice, theology as *Wissenschaft* and church training, state university and church, and between human culture and obedient Christian discipleship as two autonomous equals. His proposal was to mediate between the tension between Christianity as distinctive religious community, which is characterized by certain ritual forms and institutions, a common scripture, and its memory of Jesus as the founder and the image of God, and Christianity as an official institution in the general cultural network of social and intellectual attitudes and arrangements. Both approaches to

---

8   Frei, "Theology in the University," in *Types*, 113. Under Schleiermacher's adjudication, there is no supertheory by which to mediate between external descriptions and Christian self-descriptions; they are correlated directly from their own autonomous base. There is a direct correlation of internal and external descriptions of the essence of Christianity, the first-order religious discourse about the self-consciousness of Jesus in relation to the feeling of absolute dependence, in which they mutually illuminate the semantic convergences but without surrendering their distinctions under a totalizing theoretical account that mediates as a supertheory. This direct method of correlation is maintained in the relation between theology and philosophy. Schleiermacher thought that moral philosophy and metaphysical reflection led to an idea of a transcendent ground of all being and action, to which we are immediately related in the experience of ourselves as absolutely dependent, but this inevitable idea is elusive and not simply made explicit in general and without attention to particular human communities. So, there is a real reciprocal relationship between theology and philosophy, but clearly philosophy does not function as a foundational discipline. For further discussion on Schleiermacher's understanding of the exact nature of the relation between internal and external descriptions, see Frei's discussion on the essence of Christianity through borrowed propositions from ethics, philosophy of religion, and apologetics. Frei, "Barth and Schleiermacher," in *Theology and Narrative*, 192-194.

Christianity are considered not as necessarily in conflict with each other but as distinct and autonomous realms that are to be brought together in a non-reductionistic dialectical resolution.[9]

C. Lessons from the Case of Berlin

To cull some basic insights from this investigation, there are questions worth considering. First of all, whether situated in a Christian institution or a university setting, how do mission studies programs account for the irreducible Christian specificity of the enterprise? This question may not be avoidable whether the faculty is carrying out participatory internal Christian self-description or external social scientific description. It may be the case that the former uses distinctive concepts that inform the Christian community and while using them she also describes them; the latter describes the concepts without using them; and the difference between the two is one of practice and judgment. If we grant Christianity to be in the first place a socio-linguistic culture of a religious community with informal, practical rules and conventions that govern the semiotic system, one way to conduct mission studies is as a native who has learned to use its grammar as in a language game, and another is as an outside social anthropologist giving voice to the agent's point of view in empirically minded ethnographies (Frei 1992: 12-14). In either case, mission studies entail providing thick descriptions that explain the publicly instantiated internal logic of communal language and action concerning its mission, such as the *missio Dei* or the reign of God (Frei 1992: 135).[10]

---

9   Frei notes that Schleiermacher sought to maintain "genuine continuity with the church's understanding of scripture and to correlate external description and internal description in light of the culture despisers of religion." Frei, "Some Implications for Biblical Interpretation," in *Types*, 66.

10   Frei quotes Geertz, "As interworked systems of construable signs ... culture is not a power, something to which social events, behaviors, institutions or processes can be causally attributed; it is a context, something within which they can be intelligibly—that is, thickly—described." Frei, "The 'Literal Reading,'" in *Theology and Narrative*, 146. On the importance of providing thick descriptions of socially established structures of meaning from the actor's point of view in social anthropology, see Clifford Geertz, *The Interpretation of Cultures*, 6-20. For a fascinating exposition of Geertz's understanding of culture as a semiotic system with conventions and rules, see

Secondly, whether or not one undertakes mission studies as an internal, participatory process, it cannot be reduced to Christian self-description leading to a sectarian retreat precisely because of its citizenship in the academy. It must simultaneously maintain Christian self-description and academic inquiry that correlates between theology and *Wissenschaft*.[11] There may be some truth to Frei saying that "despite qualifications and caveats, the problematic and the span of theological possibilities represented by Schleiermacher's so-called mediating theology ... are our concern" (Frei 1992: 120). And taking up mediating theology would mean doing constructive theology in an *ad hoc*, eclectic mode of bricolage that maintains theology as both Christian self-description and academic inquiry. As shown above, Schleiermacher opted for a position that is clearly related to the universe of thought and discourse under general rules of coherence, meaningfulness, and faith, but it is also a conceptual skill governed by practical aims in a specific context, i.e., as the church (Frei 1992: 114). There is an attempt to follow both the general rules of intelligibility and the intelligent agent's social aim. Just as he had eclectically organized the disciplines of the university, the relation between *Wissenschaft* and theology is understood as one of direct correlation rather than strict identification.

Thirdly, what exactly is the nature of the relation between mission studies in the academy and external institutional-cultural aims of the church that are practical and social in character? Coming to terms with professionalization in mission studies would mean defining clearly the nature of the relation between the practical/professional character of Christian missions and its curriculum, faculty selection, and student employment in the public domain. Depending on the identity of the school, mission studies program may or may not be closely aligned with the practical/professional understanding of Christian missions nurturing its ties to the church, mission agencies, and non-profit organizations. In programs with close institutional ties, the issue would, at least, be partially resolved by articulating how it trains its students as professionals in the modern sense to integrate theory and praxis in order that they acquire the requisite skills and competencies for carrying out practical work in

his essays "Person, Time, and Conduct in Bali," and "Deep Play: Notes on the Balinese Cockfight." On Frei's discussion of the hermeneutics of restoration, see Frei, "Introduction," in *Types*, 12-13.

11 Frei observes different configurations, such as between two autonomous, distinctive discourses, or by recognizing the rightful status of one through the priority of the other, or even determining that the two are in principle absolutely different and there can be no real contact between them." Frei, "Types of Academic Theology," in *Types*, 118.

mission related institutions. In such cases, nurturing those distinctive conceptual skills needed for the professional response to practical and social challenges in varying contexts deserves attention. This involves imparting and acquiring "the grammar, internal logic, or the first-level statements kept alive in the church" attuned to both the continuities and changes in its norms, patterns, and conventions, and providing second-level descriptive and critical appraisals of its first-level language and practices. And further still, it may also accompany the art of expressing Christian affections in kerygmatic, poetic, and rhetorical forms as well as demonstrating the skills of governance.

And lastly, one of the critical implications of following a social scientific approach to mission studies is orienting one's program to the socio-linguistic community called the church and especially the missional context of ordinary Christians in the public sphere of the society. Attention to the real, concrete world of ordinary Christians in the public world permeated Frei's entire work, and toward the end of his career, he sought to do social history from pew-level of the masses of ordinary churchgoers (Higton 2004:185-186). His turn toward ordinary lives of Christians can also be seen in his work with Marxist criticism to deepen the link between the subject and the socio-political realities of the public world. Frei wrote, "Marx understood far more clearly than Feuerbach that man (including his thinking) exists both as the moving, dialectical relation of individual and society and as the conjunction of culture with material nature" (Frei 1993: 250-256). This Marxist insight into the dialectical interplay between the character and social structures reinforced his understanding of the public character of religion in the realm of concrete history of ordinary people where Jesus identified incognito with the poor, the undeserving, the spiritual and economic underclass.

In that light, the question "What's in a name?" is perhaps best answered by another familiar question "Who is my neighbor?" Jesus answered the question using a parable that stirred the hearts and minds of the listeners about the other and the different. Likewise, we fire up our poetic imagination to experiment with mission studies titles and programs to bear the imprint of our neighbors, regardless of their race, class, and gender, whom we may not prize but they are God's treasures.[12]

---

12   H. Richard Niebuhr writes, "The self we loved is not the self God loves, the neighbors we did not prize are his treasures, the truth we ignored is the truth he maintains, the justice which we sought because it was our own is not the justice that his love desires." H. Richard Niebuhr, *The Meaning of Revelation* (Louisville, KY: Westminster John Knox Press, 2006), 99.

Works Cited

Frei, Hans W.
    1974   *The Eclipse of Biblical Narrative.* New Haven: Yale University Press.

    1992   *Types of Christian Theology.* New Haven: Yale University Press.

    1993   *Theology and Narrative: Selected Essays.* New York: Oxford University Press.

    1997   *The Identity of Jesus Christ.* Eugene, Ore.: Wipf and Stock Publishers.

Geertz, Clifford
    1973   *The Interpretation of Cultures.* New York: Basic Books.

Higton, Mike
    2004   *Christ, Providence and History: Hans W. Frei's Public Theology.* London: T & T Clark.

Niebuhr, H. Richard.
    2006   *The Meaning of Revelation.* Louisville, KY: Wesminster John Knox Press.

Ricoeur, Paul
    1984   *Time and Narrative.* Vol. 1. Chicago: University of Chicago Press.

    1992   *Oneself as Another.* Chicago: University of Chicago Press.

Tracy, David.
    1981   *The Analogical Imagination.* New York: The Crossroad Publishing Company.

Woolverton, John
    1993   *Anglican Theological Review* 75, no. 1 (Winter 1993).

The Viability of the Doctor of Missiology Degree

(The DMiss is dead; Long live the DMiss!)

RICHARD L. STARCHER

DOI: 10.7252/Paper. 000054

About the Author

After pastoring in Nebraska for four years, Rich Starcher served 24 years with the Evangelical Free Church Mission in Africa. He holds graduate degrees from Trinity Evangelical Divinity School, the Faculté Libre de Théologie Evangélique à Vaux-sur-Seine, Carey Theological College (Vancouver, BC), and the University of Nebraska at Lincoln. He presently serves as Associate Dean and Professor of Intercultural Education & Missiology at Biola University's Cook School of Intercultural Studies. Rich also edits *Missiology: An International Review.*

Abstract

The Doctor of Missiology degree (DMiss), unlike its more prosperous cousin, the Doctor of Ministry (DMin), has seen a decline in enrollment in some institutions and has been eliminated from the program offerings of others. Its utility and viability are in question.

This paper discusses the DMiss's place in the array of missiological doctoral programs, explores factors contributing to its viability, scope and content, and revisits its name. Data were collected from the seven institutions still offering an accredited DMiss degree in North America. This quasi-professional degree program is compared to both the DMin and the PhD in Intercultural Studies offered at the same institutions.

Two viability factors emerged from the data: 1) program focus and 2) achievability. Program focus impacted admission standards, program relevance, and the program's capstone piece (i.e., dissertation or ministry project). Achievability concerned accessibility, affordability, and program length.

The following suggestions were made for revitalizing an institution's Doctor of Missiology program: 1) sharpen the program's focus by targeting students who are working professionals and by offering specialized tracks that leverage prospective students' areas of interest; and 2) make the program more accessible, less expensive, and shorter in order to differentiate it more from the related PhD degree in Intercultural Studies. The paper concludes with recommendations for further research.

Introduction

The Doctor of Missiology (DMiss) degree came into existence in the 1970s as missiology was establishing itself as a distinct discipline (Martin 1974). The same time period saw the launching of the American Society of Missiology and *Missiology: An International Review* (Milner 2005). While the society and journal continue to prosper, the degree has been in decline in the United States since the mid 1990s as cognate PhD programs have replaced them (Starcher 2003). Is the DMiss degree a relic of a bygone era or does it still have some life in it? If it is useful, what is its function? Who is it for? What should it look like?

Some institutions, like Trinity Evangelical Divinity School and Asbury Seminary, phased out their DMiss programs when or after introducing their PhD in Intercultural Studies. However, others, such as Fuller Seminary, Southern Baptist Theological Seminary, Assemblies of God Theological Seminary, and Biola University, continue to grant both degrees.

This study sought to discover and describe factors affecting and shaping a viable DMiss program; that is, a program that students find meaningful and attractive enough to keep enrollment numbers at a level justifying the program's continued existence. This study analyzed data collected from archival documents (including institutions' websites and course catalogs) and through semi-structured interviews with leaders from four institutions. It is limited to DMiss programs in North America accredited by the Association of Theological Schools (ATS) or by one of the eight regional accreditation bodies.

The DMiss degree shares characteristics of other "professional" doctorates, like the Doctor of Psychology (PsyD) and the Doctor of Education (EdD). The viability of such professional doctorates has been debated, particularly in the case of the EdD (Starcher 2010). This study contributes to the literature on professional doctorates in general and serves as an example of program evaluation of graduate programs of questionable viability.

DMiss Degree's History and Purpose

The purpose of the DMiss degree is intertwined with its history. From its earliest years, there was tension between the degree's professional and academic orientation. This tension continues to the present day, however, such tension is not limited to degrees in missiology but extends to degrees such as the EdD (cf. Starcher 2003, pp. 98-99).

Professional versus Academic Doctorates

Traits often associated with an academic doctoral program include: stringent admission requirements (e.g., a high GPA and/or GRE score, an acceptable sample of academic writing, multiple foreign languages), program length (e.g., a minimum of four years of fulltime study), comprehensive examinations, approximately 20 percent of the program devoted to research methods and production, and a scholarly dissertation (as opposed to a research project). While not all academic doctoral programs manifest all these traits, the traits provide a basis of comparison (Starcher 2010).

The Evolution of the DMiss Degree

According to Milner (2005), Fuller Seminary's School of World Mission began offering North America's first Doctor of Missiology degree in 1970. It was a rigorous professional degree of 96 quarter-units past the Master of Divinity (MDiv) degree (equivalent to 64 semester-units). Modeled after the Doctor of Education (EdD) degree, it was described as "a professional degree requiring a great deal of research rather than a research or academic degree" (Milner 2005, p. 63). Milner cited the following excerpt from the school's January 1972 faculty minutes.

> It fits men [sic] to administer missionary societies, train leaders of younger Churches, solve the crucial problems of modern missions, plan advances, think strategically and biblically about mission, and in short, to be more effective missionaries in the era of great advance now in progress. (Milner 2005, p. 68)

When Trinity Evangelical Divinity School began offering the DMiss degree in 1977, its program closely resembled the professional Doctor of Ministry degree, however, by 1987, in order to receive ATS accreditation, TEDS had "upgraded" its DMiss from 48 to 72 (quarter) credit hours, which made it parallel to its EdD (Milner 2005). Subsequently, "the development went ahead to the Ph.D. in Intercultural Studies, the professional was moved to the D.Min. in Missiology" (Milner 2005, p. 91).

> By 1993 [TEDS's] D.Miss. had become an "academic" degree, incorporating… additional credit hours, three foreign languages, a scholarly dissertation, three times as many research courses, written and oral comprehensive examinations, and more stringent admission standards. The step from the academic D.Miss. of 1993 to the Ph.D. in Intercultural Studies of the following year was small, involving only slightly higher admission requirements. (Starcher, 2010 p. 37)

Meanwhile, Fuller retained both the Ph.D. in Intercultural Studies and the Doctor of Missiology. The most obvious difference between the two degrees at Fuller in the late 1990s was the number of required credit hours:

> 56 for the Ph.D. but only 48 for the D.Miss. (identical to Fuller's D.Min.). Other indices of increased academic rigor for the Ph.D. program included more stringent admission standards and one additional comprehensive examination. Perhaps the most important difference between Fuller's two missiology programs was their respective stated purpose: professional certification for the D.Miss. versus academic certification for the Ph.D. Nevertheless, both

programs comported many of the same "scholarly" traits; namely, evidence of writing competence for admission, comprehensive exams and a scholarly dissertation (as opposed to a ministry project). Both programs also required three years of relevant vocational experience for admission. (Starcher 2003, p. 117)

At this juncture, a review of the existing DMiss program in North America is instructive. The degree has morphed since its earliest days. An interesting recent development involves nomenclature.[1] Since 2012, at least three institutions have changed the name of the degree from Doctor of Missiology to Doctor of Intercultural Studies. A fourth, Fuller, allows graduating students to choose between having Doctor of Missiology and Doctor of Intercultural Studies on their diploma and transcript.

North American Institutions Offering the Doctor of Missiology Degree

I found only seven North American institutions offering a DMiss degree (or equivalent) with Association of Theological Schools (ATS) and/or regional accreditation: 1) Andrews University, 2) Assemblies of God Theological Seminary (AGTS), 3) Biola University, 4) Fuller Seminary, 5) Grace Theological Seminary (GTS), 6) Southern Baptist Theological Seminary (SBTS), and 7) Western Seminary. Of these insti-

---

1   The ATS website presently lists two schools accredited to offer the DMiss degree: Asbury Theological Seminary, and Southern Baptist Theological Seminary. Asbury no longer offers the DMiss degree. Fuller is not listed, but the omission appears to be an oversight. Grace Seminary's and Western Seminary's degrees (formerly DMiss) are now listed as Doctor of Intercultural Studies. AGTS's degree is now listed as :Doctor of Applied Intercultural Studies." Biola University's DMiss program has regional but not ATS accreditation because it is housed in Biola's School of Intercultural Studies rather than its School of Theology.

tutions, four also offer the PhD in Intercultural Studies.[2] Table 1 compares these four schools' programs. Table 2 compares the remaining three. All seven institutions offer the DMin degree.

Required Credit Hours

The number of credit hours required to earn a DMiss varied from 32 to 48 (semester) units among the seven schools. Fuller is the only institution with an academic year based on the quarter system. I calculated 48 quarter units as the equivalent of 32 semester units, using the standard rate of 1 quarter unit = 2/3 semester unit.

---

2   Andrews University offers a PhD in Religion with an emphasis in Mission and Ministry.

Table 1: Comparison of Four DMiss Degrees

	AGTS	Biola	Fuller	SBTS
Degree name	Doctor of Applied Intercultural Studies (DMiss on institutional website)	Doctor of Missiology	Doctor of Missiology (Doctoral of Intercultural Studies optional)	Doctor of Missiology
Stated purpose	Enhance missionary practice and resources; Prepare participants to teach missiology at any level; Build foundations for training missionaries overseas; Equip leaders for compassion ministries	Enhance people, partnerships and publications advancing the missions enterprise to a higher level of scholarship, spirituality, service, and sacrifice through the critical reflection of cross-disciplines: church history, theology, the social sciences, and missions strategies	Foster and equip communities of learning for in-service leaders from all parts of the world for missiological research and transformational missional practice	Serve missionaries, practitioners, teachers, and administrators by providing advanced formal education, guided reading in pertinent missiological literature, field experience, mentoring, and supervision

Delivery system	Two courses taken during each two-week session; with the project phase, degree completed in approximately 4 years	Four semesters of modular courses on campus or six semesters in-service comprising 2-week modules at extension sites	Four annual, 37-week, cohort-based modules that each include one annual, 2-week on-campus intensive	Two weeks twice per year during summer and winter terms
Matriculation degree	Masters in an appropriate theological or missiological discipline. Deficiencies may add 15-30 credits of foundational courses	Masters with 9 units Bible/ theology (missing prerequisites may increase units needed to earn the degree)	Masters with 27 (semester) combined units of theology & missiology; minimum of 9 of theology and 9 of missiology	Master of Divinity, Master of Arts in Missiology, or its equivalent from a regionally accredited or ATS accredited seminary
Credit hours	*48 semester units*: 11 courses for 44 units + 4 units final project/ dissertation	*40 semester units*: 12 courses for 36 units + 4-unit capstone project	*32 semester units*: 48 quarter-units (7 courses of 4 or 8 units + 8-unit dissertation)	*48 credit hours* including 6 for guided mentorship, 6 for dissertation writing & defense
Research tools	One 4-unit course	Two courses for 6 units	Spread throughout the program	6 hours
Final project	Project worth 4 semester units	Capstone project: 4 sem. units	Dissertation: 8 qtr (5.3 sem.) units	Dissertation worth 6 credit hours
Comps	Written	None	None mentioned	Written
Tuition	*$23,400* for the entire program	*$20,920* (40 semester units)	*$25,440* for 48 qtr units (cf. 32 sem. units)	*$36,338* for entire program
Discounts	*$18,400* for AG missionaries	None mentioned	None mentioned	$20,725 for So. Bapts & IMB

Accreditation	ATS & regional	Regional (WASC)	ATS & regional	ATS & regional
Language req.	2nd language proficiency	2nd modern language	None	2nd modern language required
Req. exper.	2 years	3 years	5 years	2 years

Table 2: Comparison of Three DMiss Degrees

	Grace	**Western**	**Andrews**
Degree name	Doctor of Intercultural Studies	Doctor of Intercultural Studies	Doctor of Intercultural Studies
Stated purpose	Prepare individuals for positive and influential leadership, relationships of trust, and biblical ministry in intercultural contexts either in denominational or interdenominational structures through study and applied learning in the socio-cultural and theological disciplines of missiology	Introduce students to the literature and resources of missiology, with special emphasis in the area relevant to the student's on-going ministry	Equip practitioners, leaders, and trainers who minister in cross-cultural mission situations through focused study and research in social-science and theological fields of study
Delivery system	One-week seminars and fully online courses	Annual cycle with each class including a week-long intensive seminar	Four cohort-based modules that includes a 4 week, on campus, residential period
Matriculation degree	MDiv degree or equivalent (i.e., 60 credit hours of graduate theological training)	Masters with 15 units Bible, 15 units theology & 15 units missiology (45 total)	MDiv degree or equivalent, or other adv. masters-level degree with 15 units mission-related
Credit hours	*48 semester units*: eleven 4-unit courses + 4 unit research project	*36 semester units*: 10 courses for 30 semester units + 6-unit dissertation	*48 semester units,* 11 courses for 42 units + 6 unit dissertation

Research tools	One 4-unit course	Two courses for 6 units	Two courses for 6 units
Final project	Research project worth 4 credits	Dissertation worth 6 units	Dissertation worth 6 units
Comps	None mentioned	Written	None mentioned
Tuition	*$19,560* ($1,630/ seminar; 12 seminars)	*$16,200* (for 36 units)	*$55,488** (for 48 credits)
Discounts	Unknown	Unknown	Unknown
Accreditation	ATS & regional	ATS & regional	Regional & SDA
Language req.	None mentioned	Field research language	2nd language for certain concentrations
Req. exper.	4 years	2 years	3 years

*Unconfirmed amount

Professional/Academic DMiss Degree

All seven programs have components associated with a professional degree program (e.g., professional experience required for admission). Nevertheless, all also comport certain attributes normally associated with an academic doctorate. Perhaps the most telling difference is the nature of a program's capstone project. While academic doctoral programs regularly require original research advancing theoretical understanding in their discipline, professional doctorates tend toward applied research projects. For example, Fuller describes its DMiss' research component as follows:

> While the main priority of traditional research is to expand knowledge, applied research seeks to utilize research in order to solve a practical problem. Students enter the DMiss aiming at a particular area in their contexts where they want to see change. (http://www. fuller.edu/academics/school-of-intercultural-studies/ advanced-degree-programs/doctor-of-missiology/ program-structure.aspx)

Western's DMiss capstone is similar to Fuller's. "The dissertation serves as a capstone project which is immediately related to the ministry of the writer" (http://www.westernseminary.edu/Admissions/Programs-Degrees/Portland/doctor-of-missiology-dmiss.htm).

AGTS calls its DMiss capstone a "project," but the director considers it more rigorous than the seminary's DMin projects. SBTS calls its capstone a "field research dissertation" and appears to strike a middle ground between its DMin "ministry project" and its PhD dissertation, which entails conducting and reporting on original research. SBTS' DMiss field research dissertation "addresses a missiological issue in [the student's] missionary context and … demonstrates a high level of research skill" (Southern Seminary 2010-2011 catalog, p. 128). Biola's DMiss recently replaced its academic dissertation with an action-reflection research project.

A comparison of various doctoral programs revealed the relative position of each doctorate on the professional-academic continuum. Assuming the DMin is universally viewed as a professional degree and the PhD is universally classed an academic degree, tables 3 through 9 (found in Appendix A) clearly demonstrate that contemporary DMiss programs occupy a position between the professional DMin and the academic PhD, however, at some institutions the DMiss has a greater affinity to the professional degree program than at others. For example, Grace Seminary's DMiss and DMin programs are closely aligned. Also, Western Seminary, which does not offer a PhD in Intercultural Studies, presents its DMiss as parallel to its DMin. The school's 2010-2011 academic catalog stated,

> The Doctor of Ministry and Doctor of Missiology programs at Western Seminary are two professional degrees with significant compatibility: a non-residence module format, field research, and the dissertation. Students enrolled in one program may cross-register for up to two electives (six credit hours) in the other. The module format of both programs is designed to make doctoral level training programs accessible to active practitioners in ministry. (p. 68)

However, the seminary's DMiss director explained that in recent years he has sought to distance the DMiss from the DMin, especially in regard to its research emphasis (personal communication).

The main "academic" distinguishing marks of Western's DMiss are its comprehensive exams, six more units of coursework, and greater emphasis on research. While Biola's DMiss formerly differed from the PhD primarily in the number of required courses, it recently lowered its DMiss admission requirements, eliminated comprehensive exams, and substituted an applied research project for its scholarly dissertation. With the exception of Grace, the remaining schools' DMiss programs have admissions requirements more rigorous than for the DMin. All require more coursework for the PhD than the DMiss but, with the exception of Fuller, slightly more for the DMiss than for the DMin. (See Appendix A for a comparison of each school's doctoral programs.)

The Vitality of Today's DMiss Programs

From 2006 (when the institution launched its PhD in Intercultural Studies) to 2012, Biola saw very few new students enter its DMiss program. During the same period DMiss enrollment at SBTS, AGST, and Western remained relatively stable, despite the presence of a PhD program in Intercultural Studies at the first two institutions. Western admits about five new DMiss students per year. SBTS has ten to twelve DMiss students at any given time; AGST has about 20.[3] At the same time, Fuller's DMiss is remarkably well subscribed. While as recently as 2007 Fuller's program was in decline, in 2012 it boasted twelve active cohorts averaging six or more students (interview data). Since revamping its DMiss program in 2012, Biola, also, has experienced a substantial influx of new students.[4]

---

3   Schools with relatively small total enrollment in their DMiss program can afford to continue offering them because DMiss students regularly take courses also offered in other programs (e.g., the PhD in Intercultural Studies). Hence, the institution's cost to run the program is negligible.

4   While only seven DMiss students matriculated between 2006 and 2011, 18 have matriculated since 2012.

Two factors emerged from the data as clearly contributing to program viability: 1) program focus and 2) achievability. Three aspects of a program's focus and three aspects of its achievability emerged as important. (See Figure 1).

Program Focus

As early as 2002, Doug McConnell, then Dean of Fuller's School of Intercultural Studies, was talking about revitalizing Fuller's DMiss.

> I asked the doctoral committee if I could have a go at rewriting the D.Miss. ... I feel like we've done such a great disservice that we need to revitalize the D.Miss... Right now Biola's got a great program and they're leading us all. (Milner, 2005, p. 135)

He added, "For a mission director, the problem with a PhD program is you send, in a sense, your best and brightest and then you lose them" (Milner, 2005, p. 135). McConnell wanted a practical DMiss program designed for students involved in fulltime mission ministry that would encourage them to stay in ministry while completing their degree. Delivery system, of course, is important to allowing students to remain in ministry. (See below, under "Accessibility.") However, program focus is equally important.

Figure 1: Important Viability Factors

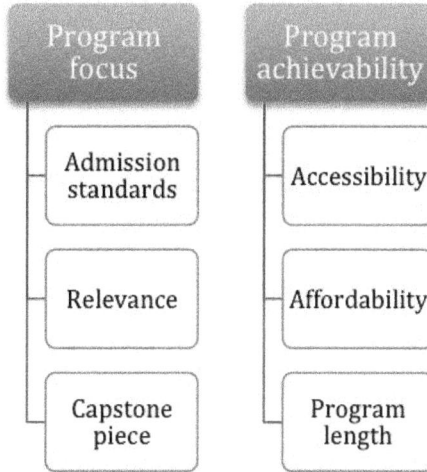

If the DMiss program's rigor resembles too closely that of the PhD in Missiology (or Intercultural Studies), it loses its unique focus. While all the schools in this study deemed the DMiss to be more rigorous than the DMin and less rigorous than the PhD, the "distance" between the DMiss and the PhD must be great enough to make the DMiss attractive to practitioners. Three aspects of doctoral program design seem particularly import to identifying a DMiss program's place on the continuum between "purely" professional and "purely" academic: 1) admission standards, 2) program relevance, and 3) the capstone piece.

Admission standards.

Admission standards reveal whom a program targets. A program targeting scholars demands a high GPA, high GRE scores, competence in multiple languages, and proof of scholarly writing capacity. A program targeting practitioners might relax the above requirements while simultaneously increasing the experience requirement. As mentioned above, ATS's published statement on admission allows matriculation with an MDiv degree or a theological master's degree, with no mention of the number of missiology courses. (Many seminaries' MDiv degree requires only one "missions" course.) Hence, it appears conceivable for a "standard" MDiv holder to enter an ATS-accredited DMiss program without missiology deficiencies to make up. At the same time, relevant field experience or self-directed learning might be counted as compensating for missiological coursework. Schools could administer "qualifying" exams at the outset or early in a DMiss program to assess students' readiness to undertake doctoral studies in missiology.

Relevance.

This theme is inferred largely from examining Fuller's revitalized DMiss program, which grew rapidly after the introduction of affinity cohorts.

> In 2006 Fuller... introduced a new approach to study for the doctor of missiology degree. Incoming students form nonresidential cohorts built on a significant commonality, and they work together throughout their four years in the program. Often students come from a common region or share a common research interest. In some instances they may come from the same mission or denomination, enhancing solidarity among the students as they work through the program. (Shaw 2010, p. 178)

Fuller's DMiss administrator explained the seminary is finding the affinity cohort approach unsustainable due to the length of time needed to gather one and the unwieldiness of running both specialized and generalized cohorts at the same time. Further, student attrition demands gathering a larger group of students before forming a cohort in the first place. Nevertheless, the affinity cohorts undoubtedly helped jump-start the revitalization of Fuller's DMiss. Further, the idea of leveraging commonality to attract and bring together students who all are engaged professionals still has merit. Perhaps offering different tracks within a DMiss program might, in part, accomplish the same goal without the problems associated with forming affinity cohorts.

Capstone piece.

Given the advent of PhD-ICS programs with delivery systems that no longer require students to abandon their ministry to pursue a degree, the capstone piece is more than ever important to the viability of the

DMiss. The nature of the capstone piece also touches on the fundamental distinction between a researcher's and a practitioner's doctorate. EdD (Anderson, 1983) and PsyD (Murray, 2000) degrees generally require a less rigorous dissertation than their PhD counterparts precisely because they are designed for practicing professionals rather than researchers. Murray (2000) quoted Peterson, former dean of Rutgers' PsyD program:

> PsyD students, he says, are trained as "local scientists" who apply the scientific method to problems in the field. Most programs require a dissertation or dissertation-like project, but students cover a wider range of topics than those allowed in PhD programs.

The designation "local scientists" also captures the spirit of a vibrant DMiss degree, whose holders also conduct local research in order to address problems in the field. While the distinction between PhD and DMiss research remains somewhat fuzzy in practice, it is important for distinguishing between those equipped for careers as informed, professional practitioners and those equipped for careers as erudite academics and researchers.

Achievability

Achievability, as addressed here, primarily concerns program length, accessibility, and affordability. While the importance of these three factors is uneven, all affect perceptions of achievability.

Program length. By length, I have in mind specifically the number of units required to earn a DMiss, including prerequisites (or co-requisites). Again, if the gap between the DMiss and the PhD is too small, students will opt for the more prestigious PhD even though a more practically oriented program might better fit their felt needs.

The ATS DMiss standard is, "the equivalent of two years of full-time study plus sufficient time to complete the culminating dissertation research project or field research project."[5] Fulltime study at the doctoral

---

5   By way of comparison, ATS' statement on the DMin degree reads, "The DMin program shall require the equivalent of one full year of academic study and, in addition, the completion of the project." The standard for the EdD

level is commonly calculated at nine units per term (rather than twelve units as is the case at the undergrad level). Hence, two years constitutes 36 semester units or 54 quarter units (excluding the program's capstone piece). Fuller's program has 40 quarter units (i.e., 27 semester units) of coursework; Western's has 30 semester units; Biola's has 36; SBTS' and Andrews' have 42; AGTS' and Grace's have 44. Given programs' various delivery systems (see Table 1), completing the coursework takes more than two academic years. Nevertheless, in terms of semester units required, the programs range from 27 to 44 semester units.

Students matriculating with deficiencies at the master's level generally are allowed to satisfy those requirements by taking additional courses in their DMiss program. Hence, program length can vary greatly depending not only on the number of units in the actual program but, also, the number of prerequisite units needed.

Among programs for which the matriculation degree is the MDiv or a master's degree in a theological discipline, the variation concerns primarily the prerequisite missiology units. Two specifically require 15 units of both theology and missiology for matriculation. The language on Western's website mirrors that of ATS:

> Doctor of Missiology program applicants shall hold either a Master of Divinity degree or a two-year master's degree in appropriate theological and missiological disciplines from an institution accredited regionally and/or by the Association of Theological Schools (ATS) in the United States and Canada.

However, when asked how many prerequisite units his program required, Western's program director told me, "According to ATS rule and according to our own MA program, at least 15 credits, semester credits, in Bible, 15 in theology, and 15 in mission."

---

degree reads, ". . . the equivalent of at least two full years (four semesters or six quarters) of academic course work and, in addition, the completion of the doctoral project." The PhD standard reads, ". . . the equivalent of two years of full-time coursework and sufficient time to prepare for comprehensive examinations, to acquire teaching skills, and to conduct the research for and writing of a doctoral dissertation."

All programs require theological prerequisites, but only three programs specifically require prior graduate studies in missiology. The total number of prerequisite units varies from 9 (Biola) to 60 semester units (Grace). Those holding an MDiv or equivalent could enter four of the seven DMiss programs without deficiencies.

Accessibility.

Undoubtedly, Biola's early adoption of a modular delivery system was what prompted Doug McConnell to remark, "Biola's got a great program and they're leading us all" (Milner, 2005, p. 135). Moving from a residential to a modular format was crucial to the revitalization of Fuller's DMiss program.

> A strength of the nonresidential-cohort approach to doctoral study is that it enables students to remain within their ministry context while completing their studies. They can both continue in ministry and obtain a doctoral degree. Each cohort meets yearly for an intensive two-week seminar facilitated by School of Intercultural Studies faculty. Twice during the program the students travel to Fuller's campus in Pasadena; the seminars during the other two years may be held at predetermined sites germane to the purpose and goals of the cohort. (Personal communication)

Fuller's requirement of only two campus visits during the whole of the DMiss program while tailoring the remaining two seminars to the various cohorts is an example of a creative delivery system that addresses issues of community and collegiality. Other approaches might combine face-to-face meeting and intentional efforts to build community online.

Affordability.

If the DMiss program is to attract working professionals who plan to continue their relatively low-paying work, affordability seems an essential aspect of program viability. Tuition costs for doctoral education at the seven schools in the study varied greatly both from school to school and from program to program within the same school. (See Appendix A.) Across the board, total tuition for the DMiss was higher than for the DMin and far lower than for the (longer) PhD. Further, AGTS and SBTS offered substantial tuition discounts to missionaries serving under the mission boards of their respective churches, however, tuition costs are only one aspect of affordability (Starcher, 2006). Equally important is a delivery system (see above) that allows students to continue earning while they are learning. Also, for non-denominational schools, partnerships with mission organizations willing to help fund their workers' doctoral education can benefit everyone.

Revitalizing a Doctor of Missiology Program

In this section, I attempt to apply the findings documented above to the viability and vitality of the Doctor of Missiology degree in North America. At the outset of this paper, I questioned the degree's viability, usefulness, function, clientele, and nature. I believe two initiatives are required to ensure the degree's viability and vitality: 1) sharpening the program's focus, and 2) increasing the program's achievability.

Sharpening the Program's Focus

Sharpening program focus involves: 1) equipping working professionals (as opposed to academic researchers) by formulating admission requirements less stringent than for the PhD and modifying the capstone piece so that it equips "local scientists," and 2) offering specialized tracks that leverage prospective students' areas of interest combined with faculty members' strengths.

Increasing the Program's Achievability

Achievability concerns include access, cost, and program length. First, an accessible program will require a minimal residency. Ideally, students would visit campus or an extension site once per year for one to three weeks. The use of a judicious number of online courses would facilitate this delivery system. Second, the DMiss should cost no more than half of an institution's cognate PhD program and no more than 25% more than its DMin program. Third, the program coursework portion of the program likely should be around 36 semester units (excluding the capstone project), making it more rigorous than most DMin programs but substantially shorter than cognate PhD programs.

Recommendations for Further Research

This study focused wholly on North American Doctor of Missiology degree programs from an institutional perspective. It ignored several potentially helpful research topics: 1) Doctor of Missiology students' perception of their degree program, 2) the utility of the Doctor of Ministry degree in Missiology or Intercultural Studies (including a comparison to the contemporary DMiss degree), 3) the state and status of the Doctor of Missiology at educational institutions outside the USA, 4) issues surrounding international students pursuing a DMiss degree in the US, and 5) factors contributing to the recent trend toward renaming the Doctor of Missiology degree (e.g., Doctor of Intercultural Studies).

REFERENCES

Elliston, Edgar J.
   1996   Moving forward from where we are in missiological
          education. In J. Dudley Woodbury, Charles Van Engen,
          & Edgar J. Elliston (eds.). *Missiological education for the
          21ˢᵗ century.* Maryknoll, NY: Orbis Books. (pp. 232-256).

Martin, Alvin.
   1974   General areas of study constituting missiology. In
          A. Martin (ed.). *The means of world evangelization:
          Missiological education at the Fuller School of World Mission.*
          Pasadena, CA: William Carey Library.

Milner, Glen S.
   (2005) *The historical development of the doctor of philosophy in
          intercultural studies in evangelical seminaries in North
          America.* Unpublished dissertation: Trinity International
          University, Deerfield, IL.

Murray, Bridget
   2000   The degree that almost wasn't: The PsyD comes of age.
          Monitor on Psychology 31(1): 52.

Shaw, R. Daniel
   2010   Fuller's School of Intercultural Studies takes a new
          approach to Doctor of Missiology. *International Journal
          of Missionary Research 34*(3): 178.

Starcher, Richard L.
   2003   Preliminary considerations on theological
          doctoral program design in an African context.
          Christian Higher Education, 2(1): 97-123.
          DOI:10:1080/15363750390200358.

2006   Stakeholders' perceptions of institutional readiness to offer doctoral programs: A case study. *Christian Higher Education* 5(2): 183-199.

2010   *Africans in pursuit of a theological doctorate: Doctoral program design in a non-Western context.* La Vergne, TN: LAP Lambert Academic Publishing.

Van Engen, Charles
   1996   Specialization/Integration in Mission Education. In J. Dudley Woodbury, Charles Van Engen, & Edgar J. Elliston (eds.). *Missiological education for the 21ˢᵗ century.* Maryknoll, NY: Orbis Books. (pp. 208-231).

APPENDIX A

Table 3: Comparison of Two Doctoral Programs at Western

	DMin	**DMiss**
Min. GPA at admit	3.0 out of 4	3.0 out of 4
Experience req.	3 years	2 years
Other admit req.	Ministerial vocation & writing sample	Admission essay
Language req.	None mentioned	None mentioned
Research methods	One 3-unit course	Two 3-unit courses
Units to graduate	30 semester units	36 semester units
Comps	None mentioned	Written
Capstone	Field research worth 6 units	Fieldwork dissertation worth 6 units
Research emphasis	9 units total	12 units total
Program tuition cost	$13,500	$16,200

Table 4: Comparison of Two Doctoral Programs at Grace

	DMin	**DMiss**
Min. GPA at admit	3.0 out of 4	3.0 out of 4
Experience req.	3 years	4 years
Other admit req.	Ministerial vocation & writing sample	Admission essay
Language req.	None mentioned	None mentioned
Research methods	One 4-unit course	One 4-unit course
Units to graduate	36 semester units	48 semester units
Comps	None mentioned	None mentioned
Capstone	Field research worth 4 units	Final project worth 4 units

Research emphasis	8 units total	8 units total
Program tuition cost	$14,670	$19,560

Table 5: Comparison of Three Doctoral Programs at Andrews

	DMin	Doctor of Intercultural Studies	PhD in Religion: Mission & Ministry
Min. GPA to admit	3.0 out of 4	3.0 out of 4	3.5 out of 4
Experience req.	3 years	2 years intercultural	2 years intercultural
Other admit req.	Ministerial vocation	Writing sample	Writing sample
Language req.	None mentioned	2nd language	2nd language
Research methods	One 3-unit course	One 4-unit course	Three 4-unit courses
Comps	None mentioned	Written qualifying exams	Written
Units to graduate	30 semester units	48 semester units	60 semester units
Capstone	Ministry project worth 3 units	Final project worth 4 units	Dissertation worth 4 units
Research emphasis	6 units total	8 units total	16 units total
Program tuition cost	$15,900	$18,725	$35,000

Table 6: Comparison of Three Doctoral Programs at AGTS

	DMin	DMiss	PhD in ICS
Min. GPA to admit	3.0 out of 4	3.0 out of 4	3.5 out of 4
Experience req.	3 years	2 years intercultural	2 years intercultural

Other admit req.	Ministerial vocation	Writing sample	Writing sample
Language req.	None mentioned	2nd language	2nd language
Research methods	One 3-unit course	One 4-unit course	Three 4-unit courses
Comps	None mentioned	Written qualifying exams	Written
Units to graduate	30 semester units	48 semester units	60 semester units
Capstone	Ministry project worth 3 units	Final project worth 4 units	Dissertation worth 4 units
Research emphasis	6 units total	8 units total	16 units total
Program tuition cost	$15,900	$18,725	$35,000

Table 7: Comparison of Three Doctoral Programs at Biola University

	DMin (Talbot)	**DMiss** (Cook)	**PhD in ICS** (Cook)
Min. GPA to admit	3.0 out of 4	3.0 out of 4	3.3 out of 4
Experience req.	3 years ministerial	3 years cross-cultural	3 years cross-cultural
Other admit req.	2-page statement	None mentioned	Writing sample
Language req.	None mentioned	2nd language	2nd language
Research methods	None mentioned	Two 3-unit courses	Four 3-unit courses
Comps	Oral	None	Written
Units to graduate	36	40	60
Capstone	Thesis-Project	Action research project worth 4 units	Scholarly dissertation worth 6 units

Research emphasis	Varies	10 units total	18 units total
Program tuition cost	$12,000	$20,920	$56,760

Table 8: Comparison of Three Doctoral Programs at Fuller

Fuller	DMin (SOT)	DMiss (SIS)	PhD in ICS (SIS)
Min. GPA to admit	3.0	3.4	3.7
Experience req.	3 years	5 years "missional"	Not specified
Language req.	Hebrew or Greek	None mentioned	None mentioned
Other admit req.	None mentioned	None mention	Qualifying exam
Research methods	One 2-unit course	One 4-unit course	Four courses
Units to graduate	48 (quarter units)	48 (quarter units)	64 (quarter units)
Capstone	Ministry paper worth 6 units	Applied field research worth 8 units	Scholarly dissertation
Research emphasis	8 units total	12 units total	Unclear
Program tuition cost	$18,000	$23,250	$45,760

Table 9: Comparison of Three Doctoral Programs at SBTS' Billy Graham School

	DMin	DMiss	PhD in ICS
Min. GPA at admit	3.0	3.2	3.5
Experience req.	3 years	2 years	None mentioned
Language req.	None mentioned	None mentioned	2 research languages

Other admit req.	None mentioned	Qualifying exam	GRE
Research methods	One 2-unit course	6 units	One 2-unit seminar
Units to graduate	32 semester units	48 semester units	66 semester units
Comps	None mentioned	Written exam	Written exams
Capstone	Ministry project worth 6 units	Field research worth 6 units	Scholarly dissertation worth 16 units
Research emphasis	8 units total	12 units total	18 units total
Program cost	$13,800	$32,000	$44,400

Our Digital Footprint:

Protecting the Next Generation of Field Personnel

KAREN ANN TREMPER

DOI: 10.7252/Paper. 000055

About the Author
Karen Ann Tremper is a Professor and Director of Global Life at Life Pacific College. Served with Wycliffe Bible Translators and YWAM and is an ordained minister in the Foursquare Church.

Abstract

We live in a global community that continues to become exceedingly smaller. As universities and colleges face the challenges of preparing students to "go to the ends of the earth" it has become evident that providing outstanding curriculum is not the only aspect of preparation they must consider. The specific language used to promote their programs must be adjusted since their audience has expanded well beyond their perspective or current students.

Internet access has allowed the global community to visit universities and their program offerings online. As degree programs seek to neutralize their language a further element that must be addressed is the extracurricular programs that supplement student learning. The issue more precisely is the digital footprint that is left by the university and students themselves through social media, not limited to the university's website. This digital footprint, if not properly neutralized, can have ramifications in the future for a student whose heart is for the mission field.

This paper seeks to address the need to consider changes in the language used to describe extracurricular programs as well as the use of social media and its potentially damaging digital footprint on the future of the next generation of field personnel.

Introduction

"The Internet is at once a world-wide broadcasting capability, a mechanism for information dissemination, and a medium for collaboration and interaction between individuals and their computers without regard for geographic location" (Leiner et al. 2001, 1). The revolution of the ability to communicate via the Internet has made it possible for the establishment of a global community. From the late 1960's with the onset of the Internet to the early 1990's with the launching of the World Wide Web, communication to a larger global audience has become a reality.

The ability to communicate to the global community has not been lost on the church as it has seen the potential "to go to the ends of the earth"[1] without ever leaving the comforts of home. The challenge faced in being able to communicate freely in this global environment is that one cannot always control the audience. The explosion of technological advancement and the ability of people the church perceives as their audience to now engage in the global dialogue has forced universities and colleges to consider the language they use to promote their programs and course offerings. In addition, these institutions must consider how they will neutralize the language of extracurricular programs that supplement student learning including the use of social media. The issue more precisely is the digital footprint that is left by the university and students themselves, which if not properly neutralized, can have ramifications on the future of a student who desires to work outside of this country.

This paper seeks to address the need to consider changes in the language used to describe extracurricular programs and the resulting digital footprint, and will conclude with suggestions programs can incorporate to reduce a potentially damaging digital footprint on the next generation of field personal.

Our Digital Footprint

The Internet has provided the world with rapid access to information. This ability has been seen as a great advantage to declare the good news as it "enables new forms of social relations, new ways of networking, and new ways of organizing social, cultural, and political life" (Cheong et al. 2012, vii-viii). The new missiological strategy that emerges is one that specializes in online media that would allow Christians to evangelize and "to do mission without having to leave their full-time job or relocate" (Vu 2011). Walter Wilson, the CEO for Global Media Outreach, stated in 2011 that

---

1   Cf. Acts 1:18

by 2015[2] there would be WiFi everywhere and "we are the first generation in all of human history to hold within our hands the technology to reach every man, woman and child on the earth by 2020. . . Our generation has within its grasp everything that is required to fulfill the Great Commission" (Vu 2011). This seems to be good news when considering the Great Imbalance of field personal working among the unreached people groups versus reached people groups (Winter and Hawthorne 2009, 543). Thus it makes sense where countries have limited access and minimal personnel to use the potential of technological advances to reach them.

From this perspective the new mission field is a virtual one where online missionaries interact with people around the globe. Social media sites are the "tools to spread the Gospel like never before" (Young 2013, ii). Facebook, Twitter, Instagram, YouTube, and blogging are all vehicles used for the creation of a virtual community in which one can be invited by you or ask you to be their friend or they become a follower. Your success as a member in the virtual community is based on the number of friends or followers you have. But one must be cautious with regards to who is following or becoming your friend in your network. This produces challenges for students participating in short-term cross-cultural experiences called mission teams. The way they stay in touch with friends they made on their trips is to friend them on Facebook. All friends and followers are not always what they appear to be.

Christians are not the only ones who see the Internet, and in particular social media, as a vehicle for revival or revolution in the global community. Uprisings referred to as the Arab Spring were driven not with rifles and weapons but iPhones linked to social media sites. "The medium that carries the message shapes and defines as well as the message itself. The instantaneous nature of how social media communicate self-broadcast ideas . . . explains in part the speed at which these revolutions have unraveled, their almost viral spread across a region" (Beaumont 2011, 3). Since governments tightly control and censor Internet use, and thus social media sites, they have the ability to block their usage. However, in the case of the uprisings of Spring 2009, it was the ability of Facebook to share video and images and "users were able to transmit news bites that would otherwise never make it to mainstream news media" (Beaumont 2011, 7). As a result, those around the globe could express solidarity by their likes on a Facebook page.

---

2   This prediction has proven to be true as students studying abroad around the world with Life Pacific College are able to access courses in an online format using WiFi.

It is clear that many groups capitalize on the interconnectivity of a globalized world. The question is what information should be listed on their sites. For programs sending teams from colleges and universities in relationship to field personnel it would be difficult "to survive without the Internet and electronic interconnectivity, but they are also limited by it. Opposition has been mounted against Christian workers based on what anti-Christian extremists have learned about the plans of agencies from the agencies' websites" (Pocock, Van Rheenen, and McConnell 2005, 26). Institutions cannot be naïve in terms of their programs or the development of students via experiential learning opportunities. Not only must those who oversee departments which supplement a student's educational experience with learning opportunities around the globe be aware of necessary security measures for the student, but also take into consideration the ramifications student teams and their global interconnectivity could have on the long term field worker.

Beginnings of Security Measures

Issues of security are not new. Wycliffe Bible Translators (WBT) and Summer Institute of Linguistics (SIL)[3] are a good example of the early strategies to protect those on the field. The sister organizations were "two parts of one focus—providing Scripture in mother tongues to people without God's Word" (Franklin 2003, 7). WBT is the home organization, organized around the country of origin, which provides for the care of its members[4] and voice in the local church. SIL members are assigned to field branches in specific countries. SIL, which began in 1934 as a summer training program, was not seen as a mission organization whose focus was evangelism but a "non-profit, scientific educational organization of Christian volunteers that specializes in serving lesser-known language communities around the world. . . [seeking] to understand their culture and learn their language" (Franklin 2003, 9). Membership in SIL provided a more acceptable explanation in non-Christian environments.

---

3   My husband and I were translators with WBT/SIL from 1984-1994 working among the Eastern Keres Pueblo Indians in New Mexico.

4   WBT has a number of supportive departments to aid those serving on the field. Its structure provides aid to the field personal by reducing some administrative tasks (Franklin 2003, 7-8).

Christian colleges and universities have made name changes to their institutions as well as specific programs. Much of the logic for these changes in nomenclature is similar to that of WBT and SIL, which is to protect their graduates. Fuller Theological Seminary changed the name of one of their schools after receiving reports from their graduates "working in Muslim contexts,. . .that they could not get visas or appointed to positions that required governmental approval as soon as it was known they had degrees from a school of mission" (Kraft 2005, 237). Fuller, following the lead of Biola University[5], chose a "secular-sounding label for missiology instruction [and] in 2003 the School of World Mission officially became the School of Intercultural Studies" (Kraft 2005, 238).

L.I.F.E.[6] Bible College changed their name in 2002 to Life Pacific College. The president, Dick Scott, noted several reasons for a name change, one specifically being the "present mission realities which would allow greater access for graduates wishing to work and study abroad [as well as] denial of entrance to Muslim countries and excessive interrogation to enter [limited access countries] (Primrose 2015). This name change was met with some resistance from the college's stakeholders. After a presidential change in 2009, the new president remarked that the college's constituency would like to return to the historic name of the college. However, in discussing this with the president, he had not been aware of the layer of protection offered to LPC graduates whose goal upon graduation was long term field service[7] that the new college name provided.

Such changes in nomenclature do aid in supporting the security of graduates either returning to their home countries or those wishing to deploy after graduation. However, there are some challenges faced when these nomenclature changes occur, many of which can be attributed to histories which are no longer remembered. Many of these schools were

---

5   Biola University made changes in the 1980's regarding the name of the college as well as one of its programs Cook School of Intercultural Studies (*History and Heritage*).

6   L.I.F.E stands for Lighthouse of International Foursquare Evangelism.

7   This was a private conversation with the president of Life Pacific College after I had been asked to give oversight to the mission program on campus. The college was facing a variety of issues related to a lack of connection with the constituency within the Foursquare denomination. Thus it was suggested to reconnect with the constituency that the college return to a time where there was a strong connection which was prior to the name change.

founded as Bible institutions that were a result of a reaction against the established theological training schools in the early 1900's. As Bible institutions transitioned to accredited colleges and universities in the late 1940's the shift in focus was from training lay people to "standardizing academic programs . . . with an emphasis on training career pastors and missionaries" (Thigpen 2015, 3). When institutions begin making adjustments in their programs via changes in nomenclature the problems which emerge are issues with the constituency as suggested by the president at Life Pacific College. Charles Kraft echoes these concerns in relationship to Fuller's name changes:

> We anticipated a difficult time with our constituency if we adopted a secular name. We deemed it unlikely that the more conservative of our supporters would really understand the seriousness of the plight of certain of our students and how sympathetic we were with their problem. Indeed, we suspected that they would feel that a change of name, especially if the new name sounded "secular," betokened a move on our part toward liberalism and a loss of missionary zeal." (Kraft 2005, 237-238)

Thus as colleges and universities make adjustments in nomenclature for the protection of their graduates' future service, their historical foundations as Bible institutes may be seen in the value placed on experiential learning via the promotion of short term mission trips. The language of mission trips and mission teams is deeply embedded in the culture of Christian colleges as an important value and contribution to the mission and vision of these institutions. The challenge for this new generation of graduates is that national governments look beyond the neutrality of the student's program to the digital footprint of the institution's website as well as that of the student. This results in a need to help the constituency and supporters of colleges and universities understand that training the next generation of field personnel is still valued and students will continue to deploy to the field upon graduation. However, to protect them, it will be necessary to neutralize the language of programs that provide mission experiences.

You are being Watched

"Unlike George Orwell's novel 1984 in which only Big Brother controlled the cameras, in 2015 cheap, mobile technology has turned everyone into a watcher" (Lien and Dave 2015, A1). In a world where education abroad in any format, two weeks to a semester, is a career booster[8], experiential learning programs must coach their students how to share their experience (West 2014, 54). Students' ability to share their story is not only about issues of debriefing and re-entry but also the integration of their experiences into the flow of their lives in the United States upon their return. It is vital to engage students prior to departure for briefing and training on what of their experiences to share and how best to do so before, and after, as well as during their time abroad. No longer do students travel with cameras to capture the moments of their cross-cultural trips to enjoy upon their return to share with family and friends. Rather they use their mobile phones to connect to the WiFi and instantaneously post experiences on social media formats complete with their geographical location.

It is clear that technology is a double-edged sword. "Easy and inexpensive access to mobile services in the poorest parts of the world is now commonplace. Study-abroad administrators generally see this as a positive development for health and safety reasons" (Huesca 2013, 4). No one would suggest that for the protection of our students the use of a mobile phone is a bad idea. I make sure all my teams have mobile phone capability. However, the down side to this capability is the lack of discernment on the part of students (and faculty) with regards to their actions as they access the Internet.[9]

---

8   NAFSA: Association of International Educators creates opportunities for Americans to study abroad, participate in scholarly exchange programs, and study foreign areas and languages and supports the perspective that study outside of the country are valid items to include in one's resume.

9   Although not the purpose of this paper, the accessibility of the Internet to entertainment comes at a cost to the student's cross-cultural immersion. It is difficult to resist the temptation to check Facebook or instant message your BFF back home. Students are not present in their cross-cultural environment because they become consumed with being present in their

In looking at these issues one must acknowledge that the next generation of field personnel are digital natives. They have grown up in the midst of an information revolution and are masters at manipulating all manner of devices. However, they have not begun to understand the global implications and frankly nor have we as leaders. Changes have occurred in the way we "shop, bank, and go about our daily business—changes that have resulted in an unprecedented proliferation of records and data . . . preserved forever in the digital minds of computers, in vast databases with fertile fields of personal data" (Solove 2004, 1). Thus whether one is aware of it or not, and regardless of how adept one is at utilizing the technology at hand, one is being watched and what is seen becomes a digital footprint.

It is important to understand how information is gathered to see the ramifications a digital footprint could have on potential field personnel. A digital footprint "is a collection of detailed data about an individual [and] dossiers [footprints] are being constructed about all of us" (Solove 2004, 2). Three types of information flow, or the movement of data, are used to construct digital footprints.

> First, information often flows between large computer databases of private-sector companies. Second, data flows from government public record systems to a variety of businesses in the private sector. Third, information flows from the private sector to government agencies and law enforcement officials . . . [which has resulted in] an elaborate lattice of information networking, where information is being stored, analyzed, and used in ways that have profound implications for society." (Solove 2004, 3)

A student is often unaware that their digital footprint, which they assume to be private, increasingly flows to the government. Their footprint provides detailed records of their "reading material, purchases, diseases, and website activity [that] enable the government to assemble a profile of an individual's finances, health, psychology, beliefs, politics, interests, and lifestyle" (Solove 2004, 5). Many students communicate over the Internet using an avatar or a screen name which they feel provides anonymity, but the data in their digital footprint "can unveil their identities as well as expose all of the people with whom they associate or do business" (Solove

---

virtual community. They often stay up late into the night to engage with those in a different time zone while robbing themselves and others of an opportunity to experience and apply their education in another setting.

2004, 5). One can surmise that when relating to field personnel in limited access countries one's digital footprint could have major ramifications. Thus there is a need to help students who feel called to long term service to neutralize their footprint and for colleges and universities to use neutral language in providing opportunities for exposure and training.

These issues challenge how one understands the meaning of privacy. Up until recently an individual's personal information was kept relatively private due to its inaccessibility. With the onset of the Information Age this perspective became no longer accurate. The concern is not so much the exposure of secrets and the loss of reputation, but how information flow allows for more "increased access and aggregation of data" (Solove 2004, 149). The threat that programs must take into consideration for their students who desire to serve in limited access countries is "not in isolated pieces of information, but in increased access and aggregation, the construction of digital dossiers [footprints] and the uses to which they are put" (Solove 2004, 161).

Disclosure of government surveillance programs became something the public needed to grapple with after the former contractor with the National Security Agency, Edward Snowden, leaked their activity. The concern of this paper is not the ethical nature of government surveillance as it relates to one's privacy but more so what is being monitored—"phone use and internet use" (Rainie and Madden 2015, 1). Pew Research found "most Americans believe it is acceptable to monitor others, except U.S. citizens" (Rainie and Madden 2015, 3). But the government has the capacity to monitor the digital behavior of those found within their borders regardless of whether they are citizens or not. Communication and online activities such as, "[use of] search engines, email messages, cell phone use, activity on social media sites, [and] mobile apps" are what come under surveillance which are all aspects of what makes up a student's digital footprint (Rainie and Madden 2015, 4).

Within the United States such issues of surveillance are perceived within the notion of our overall safety and security as a nation. But what institutions must wrestle with is that the countries in which we take students have similar capabilities to monitor digital activity. It therefore becomes crucial to implement changes in programs that support experiential learning.

Simple Changes

There are three simple changes all programs can make.[10] The first is one many colleges and universities have already made by neutralizing the name of their programs. As already stated, sending students out in mission teams is a historical value for most Christian academic institutions. LPC, from its founding in 1923, has sent students out in summer mission teams with the goal of long term deployment upon graduation. The college has maintained this practice, but in 2010 created a more neutralized name for the oversight of these programs called Global Life and also ceased calling summer teams short-term mission teams and replaced it with short-term cross-cultural experiences.

A second change is to place all mission trips under the umbrella of study abroad as Global Life did in this academic year. This decision was made because study abroad is an academic program that is understood around the world. Thus, students participating in Global Life Study Abroad programs can choose from short-term cross-cultural experiences, summer internships, and semester programs which vary in length from a long weekend to an entire semester. Using the neutral and well understood language of study abroad protects an institution's digital footprint as well as that of students. It allows for some use of social media because students are connected to an academic program. A further benefit is the protection of existing field personnel who often help with teams and have to answer questions regarding why students are in the country.

The connection to field personnel is of particular significance in all Global Life programs. All experiences are set-up in relationship with global and national leaders within the Foursquare denomination. One might think that simply being a Christian college would produce red flags in limited access countries; however that is not the case. Some terms used in

---

10   Suggestions are based on conversations over the past four years with the college as well as field personnel.

programs prove to be more problematic[11]. Because of our close connection with the field, Global Life is thoughtful in how the interconnectivity of the college, students, and study abroad experiences has implications not only on our digital footprint but on that of field personnel, too. A simple Google search can provide an ample explanation for why a group of students are in a country and can be damaging to the reputation of long term field personnel as well as the student whose goal is to deploy after graduation.

Academic institutions might do an excellent job in maintaining neutrality and thus protecting the connections with field personnel, however early briefing and training is important with students to ensure the link to their digital footprint is neutral as well. Therefore, a third change programs can make is related to security briefing.

It is common practice, for the security of students in experiential learning programs, to register their students with STEP[12]. However, during the briefing or preparation for study abroad experiences additional training should be added relating to digital security. Students who feel "called to the nations" often experience that call at camps when they are teenagers. As digital natives, they are not considering their digital footprint at this point in their life. Posts on social media sites are unlikely to consist of neutralized language. Consequently it is important as a part of briefing or training for all study abroad experiences to include best practices for digital security and how to maintain a neutral identity in their own digital footprint.

It is not the goal of preparing students to create fear as they travel outside of the country, but it is necessary to help them be wise in what they say and what they post online. In training students at LPC, all security measures are placed in a metaphorical "box". A box contains a script for explaining why a student is in a country as well as helping students to create an online profile that extends beyond their short-term trips. Part of the script is a description of who a student is, why they are in the country, and what is presented regarding their identity on social networking sites. It is vital that students understand the risks of posting online as well as

---

11   Terms like "mission trip", "mission or evangelistic outreach", and "missionaries" among others create red flags.

12   STEP (Smart Traveler Enrollment Program) is a free service for U.S. citizens traveling abroad which allows them to register with local U.S Embassy or Consulates.

"accessing their personal accounts from public computers or through public WiFi spots" (Justice, 1). According to the U.S. Department of Justice, "once information is posted to a social networking site, it is no longer private. The more information you post the more vulnerable you may become. Even when using high security settings, friends or websites may inadvertently leak your information" (Justice, 2). It is important for students to avoid making critical comparisons or political statements regarding the countries they are visiting especially if they are posting those statements with a picture and have not disabled the GPS on their phones. Recently, students I was traveling with wanted to post all their pictures on a variety of social media sites and link them together with the hashtag of the name of the country and the word gangster. Although they viewed this as funny and it was innocent in nature, it did reveal their naivety regarding the security risks related to social media.

Students on short-term trips are asked to leave their laptops and tablets at home since it is very easy to access personal and confidential information from these devices. For students who are spending the summer as interns or in a semester study program, this does create a challenge. It is important for these students to encrypt communications with websites and in particular social media sites. They all must learn to use a variety of discreet communication tools to protect their digital footprint and those they are in contact with. Virtual Private Network (VPN) and Pretty Good Privacy (PGP) secures a computer's internet connection to help guarantee that all data one is sending or receiving is encrypted and secured from prying eyes. When using these tools it is necessary to use them on all devices including a student's mobile phone.

In a perfect world students and leaders would travel with a dedicated phone and tablet that contained no personal or private information. However, as a part of their box this information can be removed and stored in a password protected, encrypted, cloud storage where VPN connections can be made. Alternatively, a student can get a password protected, encrypted USB stick to carry personal or confidential documents. It is also helpful to use a pen name or avatar that cannot be linked to you except by those you chose to disclose your identity to. When students return home whether from a short term or extended summer or semester trip, it is important for them to check all their devices for malware and change their passwords.

The creation of a secure box when coupled with a neutralized program name under the umbrella of study abroad will help minimize the digital footprint of colleges and universities as well as that of students.

Conclusion

The interconnectivity of the world today has presented colleges and universities with challenges that have implications on their digital footprint as well as students who participate in experiential learning programs, traditionally called mission trips. With the greatest need for field personnel in limited access countries, it is vital that considerations and changes be made in programs to protect their digital footprints as well as those of students who would deploy after graduation.

The Internet does provide creative access opportunities in a virtual community in which one can share the good news, but this strategy does not eliminate the mandate to also physically "go to all the nations". Issues of security are not new to those who are called to the field but with the advent of the Internet it has become necessary to reassess our training for current security issues. Initial security measures have been made by many schools as they have neutralized the names of their degree programs and classes. However, security must go beyond formal learning and encompass the experiential learning opportunities in which students participate. Such simple changes as changing the name of their experiential learning programs, placing all aspects of these programs under the academic umbrella of study abroad, and helping students integrate security protocol within a secure box as they travel outside the country will aid in the reduction of a digital footprint that potentially could limit the next generation of field personnel.

Works Cited

Beaumont, Peter
    2015   Arab and Middle East unrest: The Truth about Twitter, Facebook and the uprisings in the Arab world. *The Guardian* 2011 [cited April 21 2015]. Available from http://www.theguardian.com/world/2011/feb/25/ twitter-facebook-uprisings-arab-libya.

Cheong, Pauline Hope, Peter Fischer-Nielsen, Stefan Gelfgren, and Charles Ess
    2012   Digital Religion, Social Media and Culture: Perspective, Practices and Futures. New York, NY: Peter Lang Publishing, Inc.

Franklin, Joice A.
    2003   *A Concise History of WBT and SIL* [cited March 4 2015]. Available from http://wwwkarlfranklin.com/index. php/667/.

    2015   *History and Heritage.* [cited March 5 2015]. Available from http://www.biola.edu/about/history.

Huesca, Robert
    2013   How Facebook can Ruin Study Abroad. *The Chronicle of Higher Education: 1-19,* http://chronicle.com/article/ How-Facebook-Can-Ruin-Study/136633.

Justice, U.S. Department of.
    2015   *Internet Social Networking Risks* [cited March 3 2015]. Available from http://www.fbi.gov/about-us/investigate/ counterintelligence/internet-social-networking-risks.

Kraft, Charles H.
    2005   *SWM/SIS at Forty: A History.* Pasadena, CA: William Carey Library.

Leiner, Barry M., Vinton G. Cerf, David D. Clark, Robert E. Kahn, Leonard Kleinrock, Daniel C. Lynch, Jon Postel, Larry G. Roberts, and Stephen Wolff
  2001   "A Brief History of the Internet." *Librarianship and Information Science* no. 96:3-24.

Lien, Tracey, and Paresh Dave
  2015   "You're Being Watched." *Los Angeles Times*, April 12, 2015, A1; A18.

Pocock, Michael, Gailyn Van Rheenen, and Douglas McConnell
  2005   *The Changing Face of World Missions.* Grand Rapids, MI: Baker Academic.

Primrose, Bruce
  2015 *LIFE to LPC*, April 6.

Rainie, Lee, and Mary Madden
  2015   Americans' Privacy Strategies Post-Snowden. Pew Research Center 2015 [cited April 25 2015]. Available from http://www.pewinternet.org/2015/03/16/Americans-Privacy-Strategies-Post-Snowden/.

Solove, Daniel J.
  2004   *The Digital Person: Technology and Privcy in the Information Age.* New York, NY: New York University Press.

Thigpen, Jonathan N.
  2015   *A Brief History of the Bible Institute Movement in America* [cited April 10 2015]. Available from http://www.etaworld/?bibleinstitute.

Vu, Michelle A.
  2015   Online Evangelism Ministry Reaches 687,000 in One Day. *The Christian Post* [cited April 20 2015]. Available from http://www.christianpost.com/online-evangelism-ministry-reaches-687000-in-one-day-48803/print.html.

West, Charlotte
  2014   "Career Booster--Education Abroad." *International Educator* (May/June):54-57.

Winter, Ralph D. , and Steven C. Hawthorne
    2009   *Perspectives On the World Christian Movement: A Reader.*
            Fourth ed. Pasadena, CA: William Carey Library.

Young, Matthew Aaron
    2013   *How Virtual Missionaries can best use Social Networking*
            sites to Evangelize Unbelievers and Edify Believers. Grace
            Theological Seminary, Winona Lake, IN.

APM

Conference Proceedings

Business Meeting Agenda

Association of Professors of Mission
2015 Annual Business Meeting
June 18-19 – Wheaton College, Wheaton, IL

1. Call to Order – Nelson Jennings, APM President

2. Approval of Agenda

3. Secretary/ Treasurer's Report – David Fenrick

4. Venue and dates for 2016 Annual Meeting (with ASM) – David Fenrick

5. Executive Committee Report – Nelson Jennings

6. Advisory Board Structure for the APM – Nelson Jennings

   a. It was agreed in 2012 to implement this new structure for three years and then to revisit the matter at the 2015 Business Meeting.

   b. The Executive Committee recommends that the structure continue indefinitely.

7. Publication of 2015 Papers – Robert Danielson

8. Support for International Association of Mission Studies (IAMS)

9. Merger with the Academy for Evangelism in Theological Education (AETE)

10. Remembering and Honoring of Deceased Members

11. Election of Officers for Advisory Board and Executive Committee

12. Recognition of 2015-2016 APM President Angel Santiago-Vendrell

13. Adjournment – Angel Santiago-Vendrell

Executive Committee Report

Association of Professors of Mission

2015 Executive Committee Report

Following the previous year's pattern, the Executive Committee met three times in 2014-2015: June 2014 at the University of Northwestern; January 2015 at Perkins Theological Seminary, Southern Methodist University; June 2015 at Wheaton College.

For the third consecutive year the APM Executive Committee and Advisory Board members met in January in Dallas, Texas at Perkins School of Theology. The expenses for the meeting were again underwritten by a grant that Robert Hunt, APM member and Director of Global Theological Education at Perkins School of Theology has received for designing a resource(s) for short-term mission education. We thus spent time on Friday evening with various church leaders participating in the project, then met as an APM body the following morning.

Here is the summary of the January APM leadership meeting:

– We discussed APM's roles, both actual (especially friendship and collegiality) and potential ones. (As one point of follow-up, information was gathered regarding similar associations of mission professors outside of North America. That data needs further assimilation and investigation.)

- We decided to recommend the continuation of the Advisory Board structure, since it provides continuity and much welcome breadth and depth of experience about the work of the APM. This matter that will be on the table at this year's business meeting.

- We also enthusiastically approved Robert Danielson's proposals to publish the upcoming 2015 Proceedings and to publish the entirety of the 1956-1974 Proceedings (3rd-12th biennial meetings) in his possession.

- We gave Angel Santiago-Vendrell, as First Vice President, input regarding possible nominees for Second Vice President and two Advisory Board Members

- We discussed very positively Angel's proposed working theme for 2016 Conference.

- We then discussed various particulars of the upcoming 2015 Conference at Wheaton:

    - Communication about ASM plans for Friday afternoon, so as to avoid a conflict with the end of the APM proceedings.

    - The Friday evening worship.

    - Larry Caldwell, as Second Vice President, will coordinate several particulars, especially including preparations for the parallel workshop sessions.

    - The great help that staff assistance coming from Northwestern will be in helping out with registration and related matters at Wheaton.

Respectfully submitted,

The Executive Committee of the Association of Professors of Mission

Nelson Jennings, President

Angel Santiago-Vendrell, First Vice President

Larry Caldwell, Second Vice President

David Fenrick, Secretary/Treasurer

2015 Business Meeting Minutes

David E. Fenrick

ASSOCIATION OF PROFESSORS OF MISSION

1.   The APM meeting was held at Wheaton College, Wheaton, IL.
      The meeting was called to order and opened with prayer on Friday,
      June 19, 2015, 2:15 p.m. by Nelson Jennings, President.

2.   The minutes for the 2014 meeting were submitted by David
      Fenrick, Secretary-Treasurer, and approved.

3.   The Secretary-Treasurer's financial report was submitted and
      approved.

4.   Nelson announced that the 2015 APM Annual Meeting location,
      as well as future meetings, has been selected by the ASM Board of
      Directors. The meeting location will be announced at the ASM
      Business Meeting on Saturday, June 20, 2015.

5.   Nelson Jennings presented the Executive Committee's Report
      from its meeting with the Advisory Board at Perkins School of
      Theology, Southern Methodist University, Dallas, TX, January 23–
      24, 2015. This third annual meeting was generously funded by the
      Grimes Foundation. (A special thank you to Robert Hunt for
      initiating this funding and partnership.)

a. The APM continued its contribution to a project to create educational resources for local churches participating in short-term missions.

b. The on-going partnership with First Fruits Press at Asbury Theological Seminary was discussed at the meeting. (A full report will follow later in the meeting.)

c. There was significant discussion and planning for the 2015 APM Annual Meeting.

d. A motion was made and approved to accept the Executive Committee's report.

6. Nelson Jennings reviewed the Advisory Board structure.

a. The Executive Committee recommended that the Advisory Board continue indefinitely due to its importance in advising the Executive Committee, assistance is planning and coordinating a growing annual meeting, and long-term strategic planning for APM.

b. Greg Leffel, past president, reviewed the mandate given the Executive Committee and Advisory Board by the APM membership at the 2012 Annual Meeting.

c. A motion was made and membership approved the continuation of the Advisory Board.

7. Other Business and Announcements:

a. Robert Danielson reviewed a proposal for member services and gave a report of the present partnership with *First Fruits Press* at Asbury Theological Seminary. This includes online services and paper publication of the proceedings and papers presented at APM annual meetings. The 2014 APM Annual Meeting reports and paper presentations are available from *First Fruits*. In regards to the 2013 online publication: to date there have been 5,677 downloads of papers, in addition to numerous purchases of printed copies (book) of the papers and proceedings in their entirety. To date there have been

1,152 downloads of papers from the 2014 annual meeting papers, in addition to purchases of printed copies. A significant number of those downloads have come from countries outside the U.S.

– APM holds the copyright to these publications.

– Contributions are voluntary.

– Robert Danielson and his library staff at Asbury Theological Seminary have collected, scanned, and edited all available APM meeting papers and proceeding since 1952. Robert Danielson and David Fenrick will edit these papers into a 2-volume collection.

8. Nelson Jennings presented two proposals from the Executive Committee.

a. A request from the International Association of Mission Studies (IAMS) to contribute to the international scholarship fund to its 2016 meeting in South Korea. The Executive Committee recommended a $1,000.00 gift. A motion was made and approved.

b. The Executive Committee recommended a $1,000.00 gift to First Fruits Press for its work on the publication of the APM annual meeting papers and proceedings. A motion was made and approved.

9. Nelson Jennings presented an idea presented by the executive leadership of the Academy for Evangelism in Theological Education (AETE) to discuss the feasibility of a merger over the next year. After discussion, a motion was made and approved for the APM Executive Committee and Advisory Board to discuss the idea with AETE and, if promising, present a proposal to the APM membership at the 2016 annual meeting.

10. APM noted the death of the following colleagues this past year, and their unique and enduring contributions to the field of missiology and the proclamation of the Gospel:

- Charles Forman

- Sam Moffett

- Roald Kverndal

- Siga Arles, India

- Willem Saayman, South Africa

- Sebastian Karotempre, India

11. The report of the Nominating Committee regarding the election of officers was submitted by Nelson Jennings.

    a.   Angel D. Santiago-Vendrell, Asbury Theological Seminary, was elected President.

    b.   Larry Caldwell, Sioux Falls Seminary, was elected First Vice-President.

    c.   Linda Whitmer, Johnson University, was elected Second Vice-President.

    d.   David Fenrick, University of Northwestern, was reelected Secretary-Treasurer.

    e.   The new members of the APM Advisory Board were introduced and approved:

        - Kathy Mowry, Trevecca Nazarene University

        - Rolando Cuellar, Lee University

12. Nelson Jennings thanked the Executive and Advisory Committees, as well as the presenters for their contribution to the annual meeting. He also introduced the new APM President, Angel Santiago-Vendrell.

13.   Angel Santiago-Vendrell thanked outgoing President, Nelson Jennings, and the Executive Committee for their outstanding work in organizing an excellent conference. He also presented the theme of the 2016 Annual Meeting – "Teaching Christian Mission in an Age of Global Christianity."

14.   Angel Santiago-Vendrell closed with prayer at 3:00 pm.

Respectfully Submitted,

David E. Fenrick

Secretary-Treasurer

Secretary-Treasurer's Report

ASSOCIATION OF PROFESSORS OF MISSION

Secretary-Treasurer's Report – 2015

	Credit	Debit	Balance
Opening Balance: June 19, 2014			6,391.46
Receipts			
Membership Dues Received	705.17		
Transfer from ASM (Less Conference Expenses)	1,657.23		
Book Sales	146.00		
Expenses			
APM 2014 Meeting Honorarium & Expenses		2,234.80	
Mission Studies Renewal		338.00	
Total			6,327.06

Balance at Wells Fargo Bank,
Minneapolis, MN, as of June 18, 2015: **$6,327.06**

Respectfully Submitted,
David E. Fenrick
Secretary-Treasurer

Conference Program

Thursday, June 18

2:00 p.m.   Meeting of APM Advisory Board and
               Executive Committee

4:00 – 6:00   Registration

5:45   Dinner (Wheaton Dining Hall)

7:00   Welcome and Introduction (Buyse
               Lecture Hall, Science Building)

7:15   Worship

7:45   Plenary Address – Dan Aleshire, Executive
               Director, Association of Theological Schools in
               the United States and Canada | The Commission
               on Accrediting:

                         "Naming and Numbering Education
                         for Missions: Changing Patterns
                         Among ATS Member Schools"

               Response and Discussion

9:00   Announcements, APM Informal Gathering

Friday, June 19

7:30 – 8:30 a.m.   Breakfast, including Topic Tables (senior scholars, APM Intro)

8:00-10:00   Registration and check-in available [Coray Alumni Gym]

8:30   Worship

8:45   Plenary Address – Elizabeth "Betsy" Glanville, Senior Professor of Leadership, Fuller Theological Seminary, School of Intercultural Studies:

"Changing the Name of Fuller's School of World Mission to School of Intercultural Studies"

Response and Discussion

9:45 – 10:00   Break

10:00 – 10:50   Parallel Paper Sessions

11:00   Plenary Address – Bill Burrows, Managing Editor Emeritus, Orbis Books, Former Divine Word Missionary in Papua New Guinea:

"Tensions between Being 'Catholic' and 'Roman' in Roman Catholic Missiology – And Why It Matters"

Response and Discussion

Noon – 1 p.m.   Lunch

1:15 – 2:05   Panel Discussion

                 Meg Guider – Boston College

                 Thinandavha Derrick Mashau – University of South Africa

                 Christ of Sauer – Evangelical Theological Faculty, Leuven, Belgium

2:15 – 3:00   APM business meeting

www.ingramcontent.com/pod-product-compliance
Lightning Source LLC
Chambersburg PA
CBHW031954040426
42448CB00006B/348